The Rhodesian African Rifles
The Growth and Adaptation
of a Multicultural Regiment through the
Rhodesian Bush War, 1965-1980

A Thesis Presented To the Faculty of the US Army
Command and General Staff College in Partial
Fulfillment of the Requirements For The
Degree
Master of Military Art and Science
Military History

by

Michael P. Stewart, Major, US Army
B.S., The Citadel, Charleston, South Carolina, 1998

Fort Leavenworth, Kansas
2011-02

The cover photo courtesy of the Library of Congress is that of General Dwight Eisenhower giving orders to American paratroopers in England.

Abstract

The Rhodesian African Rifles: The Growth And Adaptation Of A Multicultural Regiment Through The Rhodesian Bush War, 1965-1980, Major Michael P. Stewart

The Rhodesian African Rifles overcame profoundly divisive racial and tribal differences among its members because a transcendent "regimental culture" superseded the disparate cultures of its individual soldiers and officers. The RAR's culture grew around the traditions of the British regimental system, after which the RAR was patterned. The soldiers of the RAR, regardless of racial or tribal background, identified themselves first as soldiers and members of the regiment, before their individual race and tribe. Regimental history and traditions, as well as shared hardships on deployments and training were mechanisms that forced officers and soldiers to see past differences. The RAR is remarkable because these bonds stayed true through to the end of the war, through incredible pressure on black Rhodesians to succumb to the black nationalist groups and cast off a government that was portrayed to them as oppressive, racist and hateful. Through the end of the Bush War, 1965-1980, RAR soldiers remained loyal and steadfast to their regiment, and that must be their legacy. In the end, the values of the government were irrelevant. It was the regiment that drew these men in, and their loyalty was more to their comrades and their heritage than to any particular government or cause.

Objectives of the Art of War Scholars Program

The Art of War Scholars Program is a laboratory for critical thinking. It offers a select group of students a range of accelerated, academically rigorous graduate level courses that promote analysis, stimulate the desire for life-long learning, and reinforce academic research skills. Art of War graduates will not be satisfied with facile arguments; they understand the complexities inherent in almost any endeavor and develop the tools and fortitude to confront such complexities, analyze challenges, and independently seek nuanced solutions in the face of those who would opt for cruder alternatives. Through the pursuit of these outcomes, the Art of War Scholars Program seeks to improve and deepen professional military education.

The Art of War Program places contemporary operations (such as those in Iraq and Afghanistan) in a historical framework by examining earlier military campaigns. Case studies and readings have been selected to show the consistent level of complexity posed by military campaigns throughout the modern era. Coursework emphasizes the importance of understanding previous engagements in order to formulate policy and doctrinal response to current and future campaigns.

One unintended consequence of military history education is the phenomenon of commanders and policy makers "cherry picking" history—that is, pointing to isolated examples from past campaigns to bolster a particular position in a debate, without a comprehensive understanding of the context in which such incidents occurred. This trend of oversimplification leaves many historians wary of introducing these topics into broader, more general discussion. The Art of War program seeks to avoid this pitfall by a thorough examination of context. As one former student stated: "The insights gained have left me with more questions than answers but have increased my ability to understand greater complexities of war rather than the rhetorical narrative that accompanies cursory study of any topic."

Professor Michael Howard, writing "The Use and Abuse of Military History" in 1961, proposed a framework for educating military officers in the art of war that remains unmatched in its clarity, simplicity, and totality. The Art of War program endeavors to model his plan:

Three general rules of study must therefore be borne in mind by the officer who studies military history as a guide to his profession and who wishes to avoid pitfalls. First, he must study in width. He must observe the way in which warfare has developed over a long historical period. Only by seeing what does change can one deduce what does not; and as much as can be learnt from the great discontinuities of military history as from the apparent similarities of the techniques employed by the great captains through the ages....Next he must study in depth. He should take a single campaign and explore it thoroughly, not simply from official histories, but from memoirs, letters, diaries... until the tidy outlines dissolve and he catches a glimpse of the confusion and horror of real experience... and, lastly, he must study in context. Campaigns and battles are not like games of chess or football matches, conducted in total detachment from their environment according to strictly defined rules. Wars are not tactical exercises writ large. They are...conflicts of societies, and they can be fully understood only if one understands the nature of the society fighting them. The roots of victory and defeat often have to be sought far from the battlefield, in political, social, and economic factors which explain why armies are constituted as they are, and why their leaders conduct them in the way they do.... It must not be forgotten that the true use of history, military or civil... is not to make men clever for the next time; it is to make them wise forever.

Gordon B. Davis, Jr.
Brigadier General, US Army
Deputy Commanding General
CAC LD&E

Daniel Marston
DPhil (Oxon) FRHistS
Ike Skelton Distinguished Chair
  in the Art of War
US Army Command & General
  Staff College

Acknowledgments

This work would not have been possible without the efforts of many others on my behalf. First and always, I must thank my wife, Jennifer, for her unwavering support and sacrifice during the many long hours of research and writing that kept me away from my family. Thanks also to Dr. Dan Marston, Dr. Nick Murray, and Dr. Scott Stephenson for your guidance and counsel, and to my colleagues at the Command and General Staff College Art of War Scholars Program--Eric, Darrell, Mike, Marcus, Art and Half-Pint. I also appreciate the gracious assistance of eminent Rhodesian historian, Dr. Richard Wood, who provided maps, insight, and continued correspondence throughout this project.

I am eternally grateful to the veterans of the Rhodesian Army and Rhodesian African Rifles, many of whom I had the privilege of meeting during the course of this study. These are remarkable men whose hospitality, openness and honesty were tremendous. I only hope this work is adequate representation of a worthy and noble regiment.

Table Of Contents
Chapters

Abstract iii
Objectives iv
Acknowledgments vi
Table Of Contents vii
Acronyms viii
Chapter 1 Introduction 1
Chapter 2 Why Did They Fight? 13
Chapter 3 Phase One: 1965-1972 31
Chapter 4 Phase Two: 1972-1974 45
Chapter 5 Phase Three: 1974-1977 65
Chapter 6 Phase Four: 1977-1979 83
Chapter 7 Phase Five: April 1979-April 1981 93
Chapter 8 Conclusions 107
Bibliography 115

Figures

Chapter 1
    Figure 1. Ready for the Regiment 9
    Figure 2. Proud, professional RAR NCOs 10

Chapter 5
    Figure 1. RAR machine gunner 70
    Figure 2. RAR paras waiting for a fireforce call-up 76

Chapter 6
    Figure 1. Mrs. Rule, the widow of Lieutenant Colonel Kim Rule .. 89

Chapter 7
    Figure 1. RAR soldiers at Brady Barracks 104

Chapter 8
    Figure 1. Map of Rhodesia 110
    Figure 2. Rhodesian population, 1969 111
    Figure 3. Rhodesian Security Forces Operational Boundaries 112

Acronyms

2IC	Second In Command (Executive Officer)
ANC	African National Council
BSAP	British South Africa Police
CIO	Central Intelligence Organization
CO	Commanding Officer
COIN	Counterinsurgency
ComOps	Combined Operations
FRELIMO	(*Frente de Libertaçao de Moçambique*) Liberation Front of Mozambique
FROLIZI	Front for the Liberation of Zimbabwe
FPLM	(*Forças Populares para o Libertação de Moçambique*) Popular Forces for the Liberation of Mozambique
GOC	General Officer Commanding
JMC	Joint Military Command
JOC	Joint Operation Centre
KAR	King's African Rifles
NRR	Northern Rhodesia Regiment
OAU	Organization of African Unity
OC	Officer Commanding
OCC	Operations Coordination Committee
OP	Observation Post
PATU	Police Anti-Terrorist Unit
PF	Patriotic Front
PRAW	Police Reserve Air Wing
PWO	Platoon Warrant Officer
PV	Protected Village
RAF	Rhodesian Air Force
RAR	Rhodesian African Rifles
RENAMO	(*Resistência Nacional Moçambicana*) Mozambican National Resistance
RhAF	Rhodesian Air Force
RLI	Rhodesian Light Infantry
RNR	Rhodesia Native Regiment
RSF	Rhodesian Security Forces
RSM	Regimental Sergeant Major
RR	Rhodesia Regiment (after UDI)
RRAF	Royal Rhodesian Air Force
RRR	Royal Rhodesia Regiment (prior to UDI)
SAANC	South African African National Congress
SADF	South African Defence Force
SAP	South African Police

SAS	Special Air Service
SB	Special Branch
TTL	Tribal Trust Land
UANC	United African National Council
UDI	Unilateral Declaration of Independence
WO	Warrant Officer
ZANLA	Zimbabwe African National Liberation Army
ZANU	Zimbabwe African National Union
ZAPU	Zimbabwe African People's Union
ZIPA	Zimbabwe People's Army
ZIPRA	Zimbabwe People's Revolutionary Army

Chapter 1
Introduction

During 65 years of regimental history, men of different races with a common ideal had worked and fought together in a spirit of true comradeship and mutual esteem. In the process, a respect and understanding evolved between them which comes only to men who face conflict together and which cannot be described. Without exception, all who served with the regiment were proud of it and would testify to the unique and profound effect it had on their lives.

— Alexandre Binda, *Masodja: the History of the Rhodesian African Rifles and its Forerunner, the Rhodesia Native Regiment*

The Rhodesian African Rifles (RAR) overcame profoundly divisive racial and tribal differences among its members because a transcendent "regimental culture"-described above as a "common ideal"-superseded the disparate cultures of its individual soldiers and officers. The RAR's culture grew around the traditions of the British regimental system, after which the RAR was patterned. The soldiers of the RAR, regardless of racial or tribal background, identified themselves first as soldiers and members of the regiment, before their individual race and tribe. Regimental history and traditions, as well as shared hardships on deployments and training were mechanisms that forced officers and soldiers to see past such differences. These factors enabled the RAR to withstand the racial and tribal tensions of the Rhodesian Bush War (1965-1980) and thrive as a combat effective and competent military force. The history of the RAR provides an example of how military culture, effectively developed, can prevail over cultural clashes among groups of mixed identity.

Cultural backdrop

The RAR principally recruited from three groups of people within Rhodesia: the officer corps primarily came from the white Rhodesian population, while the ordinary soldiers and most noncommissioned officers were from the Ndebele (Matabele) tribe of southwest Rhodesia and the Shona (Mashona) tribe of the north, east, and central portions of the country.

The ability of the RAR to bring together disparate racial groups is altogether more impressive when one remembers that the Ndebele and Shona tribes fought each other shortly before the arrival of whites in the country. The Ndebele were descendants of the Zulus, who lived further south, and they arrived in the southwestern portion of what would become Rhodesia around 1837. The warlike Ndebele immediately came to dominate the relatively disorganized Shona tribes of the area, raiding villages and generally treating Shona as inferior tribes within the Ndebele kingdom. Several decades of internecine rivalry ensued, until the arrival of white settlers in 1890.[1]

The 1890 arrival of Cecil John Rhodes' pioneer column began to establish Southern Rhodesia-a British protectorate-based on mining rights dubiously granted to his British South African Company by King Lobengula of the Ndebele. Several years of sporadic fighting between the native tribes and Rhodes' pioneers ended in 1897 when the British South Africa Company defeated a tribal uprising. White settlers quickly established a government and economic system such that by 1931, most of the land and power belonged to the 50,000 whites, while the one million black Africans found themselves poor, uneducated and largely left out of the political process.[2]

The dynamics of racial and tribal differences in Rhodesia were rooted in this conflict, and were left simmering from the 19th century through to the 1961 nationalist movements. By 1961, the cause of black nationalism in Southern Rhodesia was led by the Zimbabwe African People's Union, a predominantly Ndebele but tribally mixed group. In 1963, a faction of ZAPU split off to form the Zimbabwe African National Union (ZANU), which became a predominantly Shona group. These two movements derived from the same tribal populations as the RAR, yet they were never as successful at setting aside tribal conflicts and rivalries as the RAR was. Using only their own tribal culture to guide behavior, the soldiers of the RAR most likely could not have formed a cohesive unit-ZAPU and ZANU never did. It took a more powerful culture-a regimental one-to unite these disparate elements into one cohesive unit.

The Rhodesian African Rifles: a Historical Overview

The RAR was the oldest and largest regiment in the Rhodesian army. Its roots dated to the 1916 formation of the Rhodesia Native Regiment (RNR), which fought for the British in East Africa during World War I. When the regiment stood down in 1919, a cadre of the RNR formed the Askari platoon of the British South Africa Police (BSAP). When the Empire called again, in 1940, this cadre formed the nucleus around which Lieutenant Colonel Francis John Wane built the Rhodesian African Rifles.[3] After training in Northern Rhodesia, Kenya and Tanganikya (Tanzania), the regiment deployed to Burma in 1944, where it distinguished itself in the fighting during the Arakan campaign, and again at Taungup and Tanlwe Chaung.[4]

After the Burma Campaign, Major Walter Walker (later General Sir Walter Walker KCB, CBE, DSO & bar), said of the RAR:

> The conduct of the askari, most of whom had never experienced enemy fire before, deserves a lasting tribute. Their energy and endurance on the march and on patrol through some of the worst country in the Arakan, their constancy and discipline under the stress of persistent mortar and artillery fire, and their cheerfulness throughout the appalling weather conditions, which developed in the latter stages of the operation, were beyond praise.[5]

Further praise for the RAR came from a captured Japanese officer's diary, where he noted, "[t]he enemy soldiers are not from Britain, but are from Africa. Because of their beliefs they are not afraid to die, so, even if their comrades have fallen, they keep on advancing as if nothing had happened. They have excellent physique and are very brave, so fighting against these soldiers is somewhat troublesome."[6]

After World War II, the RAR remained active, guarding Royal Air Force training bases in Rhodesia, before briefly deploying to the Suez in 1952. After the regiment returned home from Egypt, Queen Elizabeth II presented them with the Queen's and Regimental Colors on 12 July 1953.[7] The regiment deployed again, this time to Malaya from 1956-8, as part of the Federation of Rhodesia and Nyasaland fighting alongside the forces of other Commonwealth nations. While in Malaya, the RAR proved adept at jungle warfare, honing its skills hunting down communist terrorists in the southern Malayan province of Johore.[8]

After returning home again in 1958, the RAR was assigned to "duties in the aid of the civil power," and over the next several years was deployed into Northern Rhodesia and Nyasaland, where civil unrest was unraveling the Central African Federation - a British colonial administrative unit comprised of Southern Rhodesia, Northern Rhodesia and Nyasaland. With the breakup of the federation in 1963, three new states emerged- Zambia (formerly Northern Rhodesia), Malawi (formerly Nyasaland) and Rhodesia (formerly Southern Rhodesia).[9]

The RAR returned to the control of the Rhodesian Army in 1963, just as ZAPU and ZANU were beginning increasingly militant campaigns to overthrow the white Rhodesian government. ZAPU and ZANU each built military organizations, called the Zimbabwe People's Revolutionary Army (ZIPRA) and Zimbabwe African National Liberation Army (ZANLA), respectively. Rhodesia unilaterally declared independence from Britain on 11 November, 1965. From that date until 1980, the RAR served as a critical element of Rhodesian security forces, conducting hundreds of operations in the bush alongside other Rhodesian troops.

Of the RAR's performance during the Bush War, Army Commander Lieutenant General G. Peter Walls said:

> The men of this regiment are above faction or tribe or politics. They are an elite group of fighting men, both European and African, to whom the country owes an incalculable debt for their dedication and bravery. And their moral courage in the face of insidious assaults from those who would undermine their sense of purpose is nothing short of admirable. . . . But not only are they brave and efficient soldiers. Their spirited approach to their task and their *joie-de-vivre,* their sheer love of serving are an example which many would do well to emulate.[10]

When the ZANU-Patriotic Front (ZANU-PF), led by Robert Mugabe, took control of the country following elections in 1980, the nation became Zimbabwe, and the RAR became the 11th, 22nd, and 33rd Infantry Battalions of the Zimbabwe National Army. The regiment continued to serve Zimbabwe as a multicultural organization, while nationalist ZIPRA and ZANLA factions fought one another based on tribal differences and feuds. In fact, the RAR intervened in clashes between elements of ZIPRA and ZANLA in holding camps after the elections.[11] Officers and soldiers of the RAR began to leave the regiment as the command of the Zimbabwe National Army ordered the unit to sever its links to its traditions in order to incorporate the largely untrained and incompetent soldiers and leaders from ZIPRA and ZANLA into its ranks. The RAR officially disbanded in April 1981.[12]

Throughout its history the RAR served with distinction, first for the British Crown and the Commonwealth, then for its own country on its own soil, and ultimately-briefly-under the command of its former enemy, Robert Mugabe. Throughout all the changes and amidst all the competing cultural influences, the RAR remained a steadfast, professional military force. It was precisely this history and lineage that established the regimental culture of the RAR.

Symbols, Training, and Shared Hardships

The symbols, training and shared hardships in the RAR enhanced values of loyalty, pride, and discipline, as well as the importance of regimental identity over that of the individual. Symbols, such as the regimental colors and badge, embodied the history and nature of the regiment. Training and deployment bonded the individual members of the regiment together through shared hardship and accomplishment.

For any regiment, the colors are the most visible symbol of the unit's history. The RAR was no exception. When the Queen presented colors to the RAR in 1953, she publicly and permanently acknowledged the regiment and major campaigns in which it earned honors.[13] The Queen Mother concluded her speech at the presentation of the RAR colors with the following words:

> In the short history of the Rhodesian African Rifles you have proved by your service in Burma that you can hold your own in battle. By your service since the war you have shown that you carry your duties towards the Queen, the Colony, and its people, with smartness and efficiency. I know how many of you volunteered to serve in the Middle East when help was needed. By this, you have shown that you are ready to take your share in the welfare of the Commonwealth, by all these things you have won the honour of carrying your Colours. I present them in recognition of your loyalty in the past, and in the faith that you and those that follow you in the Regiment will always guard its tradition and strive to bring new honour to its name.[14]

In addition to the battle honors, the Queen's colors represented the regiment's allegiance to the British sovereign, symbolized in the crown and the interposed crosses of St. Andrew and St. George on the Union Jack.[15] The single icon of the colors provided every member of the regiment, from the commanding officer to the newest private, a reminder of exactly what their predecessors had done. "The colours emblazoned with battle honours, commemorating some of the gallant deeds performed by members of the regiment, are a visible record. They keep a feeling of pride in past and present soldiers."[16] By learning the history behind the words and symbols on the colors, as instructed during their training, soldiers understood what was expected of them and they took pride in their regiment.

If the colors embodied the history, the RAR badge displayed the truly multi-cultural nature of the regiment. This badge, devised within months of the establishment of 1st Battalion in 1940:

> consisted of the Matabele shield (I-Hawu), in brown and white, upon which was vertically placed a knobkierie (nkudu) and crossed assegais. Across the bottom left to top right was the Shona digging spear (Museve) with the narrow sharp blade and an iron pick at the base of the shaft. Crossing from bottom right to top left of the badge was the broad-bladed fighting spear of the Zulu

warrior (Umkonto). The badge was supported by a scroll bearing the inscription Rhodesian African Rifles, with black lettering on a red background.[17]

By capturing essential elements of the Ndebele and Shona cultures, the regimental badge symbolized the unity of these two historically hostile tribes within the RAR. The RAR created a new cultural symbol in which its soldiers, regardless of race or tribe, could take great pride. By breaking down the tribal barriers between individuals, this symbol allowed RAR soldiers to build loyalty, both to the regiment and between themselves.

The fighting spirit of the RAR evolved during its training and deployments. Training was tough, and shared by all members of the regiment-officers, soldiers and noncommissioned officers alike. Retired Australian Brigadier John Essex-Clark recalls his time as a lieutenant and platoon commander in the RAR, training his platoon to deploy to Malaya in 1956:

We snap-shot at moving targets many times a week. The twenty-five metre ranges were less than a hundred metres away and were used day and night. I taught my askari to aim very low, at the crotch area, so they would hit the chest in the gloom of the jungle. Within a few months every askari in my platoon could, while blindfold, strip, clean, assemble, load and fire at level targets in front of them. Their immediate action drills on automatic weapons were instantaneous and they could fix faults instinctively. They could pack up their gear and break camp at night within minutes. They could slip stealthily into ambush within seconds and most of them could hit with ease a moving 'figure' target at twenty-five metres.[18]

Training remained paramount through the Bush War, particularly on marksmanship, as most African soldiers had little experience with firearms before joining the army. In conducting training, the RAR soldiers learned the capabilities of their officers, and learned to trust them.[19]

Loyalty to officers in the RAR was paramount. In 1977, when the regiment was designated for parachute training, many of the men had never even seen an aircraft before, let alone jumped from one. Their motivation to do such an unnatural task did not come from their faith in the aircraft, parachute or any training-in the end, as one RAR officer described, it was a matter of trust between the officer and his men. After explaining how everything functioned on the aircraft and the parachute, as well as detailing drop altitudes and possible malfunctions, one officer was reminded of the simplicity of the matter when a soldier said, "*Ishe*, if you go, I will follow."[20]

The regiment deployed frequently throughout its history, particularly during the 1965-1980 Bush War while fighting ZIPRA and ZANLA. The rotation schedule during the Bush War was typically a six week deployment in the bush, followed by a ten day period to rest, recover and refit, then back out for six more weeks.[21] There simply was no time for racism in the RAR, nor was there room to accommodate tribal feuds. RAR soldiers and officers worried more about the level of training and competence of their men than tribal backgrounds. This cannot be said for ZIPRA and ZANLA. Tribal loyalties divided the two nationalist communist armies, and they proved unable to overcome their differences, even when mutual interest should have brought them together. In its heritage, symbols, training, and deployments, the RAR created an overriding organizational culture that transcended tribal and racial differences by bringing diverse individual backgrounds into a common culture.[22]

The deep sense of loyalty between officers and soldiers remains immediately apparent among former members of the regiment today. An American Special Forces Vietnam veteran and former RAR company 2IC,[23] commented that "[f]or those whites who served with African Soldiers in The Rhodesian Bush War there remains something that can best be called a 'Forever Sadness' caused by the separation after 'Independence' in the New Zimbabwe in March of 1980. I have a lump in my throat just thinking of the loss."[24]

Purpose and Conduct of this study

The purpose of this study is to explore the regimental culture of the RAR, and to trace how that culture evolved throughout the Bush War, from 1965 to 1980. The aim is to answer the question: why would a black African fight to sustain a white-rule government in Africa? Logically, there should have been little willingness among the black population of Rhodesia to fight-often against family members-on behalf of a government that offered little social or political opportunity for blacks. The answer lies in the traditions, history, and culture of the regiment. Simply put, black soldiers in the RAR did not fight for the white government; they fought out of loyalty to their regiment and to each other. This is an attempt to explore and describe the depth of that loyalty.

The author, an active duty US Army officer and combat veteran, has objectively researched the history and traditions of the RAR (particularly during the Bush War of 1965-1980) to develop this study. The difficulties of developing and training multi-cultural military organizations present very real and current challenges to the US military-in Iraq, Afghanistan, and increasingly in our expanding security cooperation role in Africa. This study offers insights into one successful historical example of a multicultural military unit, the RAR.

In conducting this study, the author interviewed over 30 Rhodesian Army veterans in South Africa, the United Kingdom, and the United States. Their memories and insights guide much of the discussion here. These veterans were mostly former officers in the RAR, although their ranks vary from warrant officer to major general and their regiments include the RAR, Rhodesian Light Infantry (RLI), Special Air Service (SAS), Rhodesia Regiment (RR), Rhodesian Army Education Corps, Grey's Scouts, and Selous Scouts. Many served in multiple regiments, some also served in other colonial regiments (such as the King's African Rifles and Northern Rhodesia Regiment), and most also served on the Rhodesian Army staff or the School of Infantry at least once in their careers. Several were company, battalion, and brigade commanders through key periods of the Bush War. The critical missing piece of this research is the perspective of the black soldiers who served in the regiment. Time and circumstance did not allow interviews with these men during this study, but future studies in this field must capture their insights.

The insights gathered from interviews are injected into the context and events of the Bush War through the five phases of that war. These phases were first introduced by Dr. J. R. T. Wood (a former Rhodesia Regiment soldier and eminent historian on Rhodesia) in his book *Counterstrike from the Sky*. The events and details surrounding developments in each phase, as they affected the RAR, are described for the benefit of a reader who may have little prior knowledge of Rhodesia or the Rhodesian Bush War. The aim is not to portray a complete picture of how Rhodesia lost the war. Other historical accounts have addressed such ideas,[25] and many of these works may be found in the bibliography. The aim of this study is simply to follow how these events and details influenced (or did not influence) change in the culture of the RAR through the war.

Where referenced, the interviews are kept confidential: that is, the names of the interviewed officers are not disclosed here. This is not at the request of the men interviewed, but in adherence to the policies of the Art of War Scholars Program at the US Army Command and General Staff College.

Figure 1. Ready for the Regiment. Intake of new soldiers at Depot RAR
Source: CE20110908G0001, former RAR officer (photo by Robal Studios).

Figure 2. Proud, professional RAR NCOs: Standing from left: Colonel C. B. McCullagh MBE, RSM N. Tumbare, Command Sergeant Major Obert Veremu, Command Sergeant Major Pfupa, Command Sergeant Major Gobe, Command Sergeant Major Kisi and CSM Kephasi

Source: Alexandre Binda, Masodja: The History of the Rhodesian African Rifles and its forerunner, the Rhodesia Native Regiment (Johannesburg: 30 Degrees South, 2007), 257.

Notes

1. Mark R. Lipschultz and R. Kent Rasmussen, *Dictionary of African Historical Biography* (Los Angeles, CA: University of California Press, 1989), 167-8.

2. J. R. T. Wood, "Countering the CHIMURENGA: The Rhodesian Counterinsurgency Campaign," in *Counterinsurgency in Modern Warfare*, eds. Daniel Marston and Carter Malkasian (Oxford: Osprey Publishing, 2010), 192.

3. Alexandre Binda, *Masodja: the History of the Rhodesian African Rifles and its Forerunner, the Rhodesia Native Regiment* (Durban: 30 Degrees South Publishers, 2007), 41; Christopher Owen, *The Rhodesian African Rifles* (London: Leo Cooper Ltd., 1970), 2.

4. Binda, *Masodja*, 64-68.

5. Owen, 63.

6. Owen.

7. Binda, *Masodja*, 109; J. R. T. Wood, *The War Diaries of Andre Dennison* (Gibraltar: Ashanti, 1989), 372.

8. Binda, *Masodja*, 115-133.

9. Binda, 169-173.

10. Binda, *Masodja*, 268.

11. Binda, 380-389. At Entumbane, the RAR stood between ZIPRA and ZANLA elements of the newly created Zimbabwe Army and prevented escalation of the fighting into a full-scale civil war. This is covered in more detail in Chapter 7.

12. Wood, *War Diaries*, 372; Binda, *Masodja*, 389.

13. Binda, *Masodja*, 225. The four battle honors earned by the RAR by 1953 were: East Africa 1916-18, Arakan Beaches, Taungup, and Burma 1944-45.

14. Her Majesty Queen Elizabeth the Queen Mother (speech to the Rhodesian African Rifles, 12 July 1953).

15. Unlike the RLI, the RAR never adapted the green and white Rhodesian President's Color to replace the Queen's color after UDI.

16. Wood, *War Diaries*, 14.

17. Wood., 13.

18. John Essex-Clark, *Maverick Soldier: an Infantryman's Story* (Burwood, Victoria: Melbourne University Press, 1991), 34.

19. CE20110913M0001, former RAR officer, interview by author, Durban, Republic of South Africa, 13 September 2011.

20. CE20110913M0001, former RAR officer, interview; CF20110920S0001,

former RAR officer, interview by author, London, England, 20 September 2011; CE20110915B0001, Former RAR and SAS officer, interview by author, Cape Town, Republic of South Africa, 15 September 2011. *Ishe* meant "sir" or "chief," and was the term of respect from RAR soldiers to their officers.

21. CE20110913M0001. This schedule was also reiterated in many other interviews with numerous former RAR officers.

22. CE20110909T0001, former RAR officer, interview by author, 9 September 2011; CF20110920S0001, former RAR officer, interview.

23. 2IC is an abbreviation for "Second in Command." In the Rhodesian Army, as in the British Army, the 2IC for a company or battalion had essentially the same duties and responsibilities as an Executive Officer (XO) in the American military structure.

24. CG20110927S0001, former RAR officer, interview by author, Portland, Oregon, 27 September 2011.

25. Such broader analytical works include J. K. Cilliers' *Counterinsurgency in Rhodesia*; Paul Moorcraft and Peter McLaughlin's *The Rhodesian War: A Military History*; J. R. T. Wood's article in *Counterinsurgency in Modern Warfare*; and Greg Mills and Grahame Wilson's *RUSI* article, "Who Dares Loses? Assessing Rhodesia's Counterinsurgency Experience," to list a few.

Chapter 2
Why Did They Fight?

The white Rhodesians refused to accept an effective safeguard mechanism [of unimpeded movement toward majority rule] and instead, in a referendum on July 20, 1969, approved republic status which will end all ties with Great Britain as well as constitutional proposals which lay the groundwork for perpetuation of white control. The white minority-4 percent of the population of Southern Rhodesia-made the decision; no more than a handful of the blacks voted. The minority of the 4.8 million blacks in Southern Rhodesia who are politically active have been expressing their opposition to the consolidation of white rule in two ways. A small segment have directly supported the liberation groups. . . . Another small group has campaigned internally to get as many Africans as possible on the voter rolls.

— US National Security Council, *Study in Response to National Security Study Memorandum 39: Southern Africa*, December 1969

When one studies the RAR's actions in the Rhodesian Bush War, one simple question surfaces along with a complicated answer: why would a black African soldier voluntarily fight to preserve a white-rule government in Africa? The above excerpt from a US National Security Study in December 1969 highlights the essence of the Rhodesian struggle as it was perceived outside of Rhodesia. Notably, a third group of black Rhodesians-those who supported the government and joined the security forces to preserve it-is not considered. According to the US National Security Council study, a "politically active" black Rhodesian had little cause to support the white Rhodesian government against the nationalist movements. Many did, however. By the end of the war, Rhodesian Security Forces boasted three battalions (nearly 80 percent of the regular army) of predominantly-black RAR, and many more RAR battalions could have been established. In addition, many of the BSAP policemen were black, and national service eventually placed black soldiers in the Rhodesia Regiment.[1]

To the RAR soldier, the regiment was a source of income, stability, and family pride-in many instances, he was doing the same job his father and grandfather had done before him. In the regiment, the RAR soldier was a respected member of a team rich in traditions and proud of its history. He was a part of a unique culture all its own. He was not a second-class citizen, nor was he viewed as inferior or incapable.[2] Leaders in the RAR-black and white-were tough, experienced, capable men who led by example and from the front, as do most good leaders in professional armies. While factors such as income, stability and family pride brought recruits to the RAR, they stayed and fought because of loyalty to the regiment and to their leaders.

Black Nationalism versus White-Rule

In exploring why black Africans fought for the Rhodesian government, one may ask its opposite question: why would they not? The seeds of black nationalism were well established by the 1960s. The white government offered little incentive, few opportunities for economic or political inclusion, and was viewed by many as a racist, colonial power.[3]

Black nationalist movements in Rhodesia dated back to the 1920s. Several incidents, including a 1948 general strike in Bulawayo, indicated a growing nationalist undercurrent within black Rhodesian society. The various movements for majority rule in Southern Rhodesia under the Central African Federation eventually became the Southern Rhodesian African National Congress (SRANC) in 1957 under the leadership of Joshua Nkomo. After it was banned in 1960, the SRANC reformed briefly as the National Democratic Party, then as ZAPU in 1961. ZAPU's agenda took a much more militant and hardline stance on immediate majority rule than its predecessors, conducting attacks on symbols of power structure and vulnerable white targets. This led to a ban on ZAPU in 1962, and the arrest of most of its leaders, including Nkomo. In 1963, Ndabiningi Sithole and others disaffected with Nkomo's leadership of ZAPU (including Robert Mugabe, Herbert Chitepo and Rex Nhongo) split off and formed ZANU, which committed itself to "a nonracial, democratic socialist, pan-Africanist state within the British Commonwealth,"[4] and pursued an even more hardline, militant movement for immediate majority rule. ZAPU and ZANU were Rhodesian manifestations of the larger black nationalist movements spreading across the African continent in the "post-colonial" period that began after World War II. By 1963, nationalist movements in Africa had swept from Algeria to Zambia, with varying degrees of successful transition.[5] As British Prime Minister Harold Macmillan famously stated in 1960, "The wind of change is blowing through this continent, and whether we like it or not, this growth of national consciousness is a political fact. We must all accept it as a fact, and our national policies must take account of it."[6]

On the surface, ZAPU and ZANU represented a revolutionary movement and were a part of the "wind of change." They promised a fundamental overhaul of the structure and governance of Rhodesia from minority (white) to majority (black) rule. They promised black Rhodesians their rightful share of the wealth and prosperity held by the tiny minority of whites under the Rhodesian system. Where that promise proved insufficient to secure support, they threatened and exacted horrific reprisals for any blacks who failed to support their struggle. Beneath the veil of good will, the true potential ugliness within the promise of ZANU and ZAPU was apparent to Rhodesia: to hand governance over to majority rule before that majority was ready to manage the country was inadvisable.[7] For Rhodesia, a quick glance north at the examples of the Congo, Zambia and Malawi provided ample evidence of the consequences of rushed majority rule. This coming wave of uncertainty and limited successful examples of transition to majority rule surely drove some politically aware black Rhodesians to defend the status quo of a stable (albeit exclusive) white government.[8]

The government of Rhodesia drew its heritage from precisely the imperial spirit of colonization and minority rule that was already obsolete. Cecil John Rhodes, the founder of Rhodesia, can quite objectively be described as the ultimate British imperialist.[9] White Rhodesia was founded upon commercial farming and mining. These industries relied on a steady supply of cheap, unskilled labor to support the endeavors of wealthy landowners and an efficient, business-friendly government to provide security as well as the economic mechanisms to maximize trade and profit. By 1961, this system had created a thriving economy that was unrivalled among African countries. It was truly the "jewel" of the continent. But a white government ruled it, and whites owned the key land. Black Rhodesians had little say in the governance of the country, they had no real vote, and they had very little share of the profitable farmland and mining properties. These issues were the fundamental reasons the militant black nationalist movement grew in Rhodesia, and they were the reasons the rest of the world refused to support the government of Ian Smith.[10]

These two sides-militant nationalism and incumbent white rule-grew increasingly polarized and vied for recruits among the black population. Military-aged black males in Rhodesia were often forced to choose their side.[11] Logically, there should have been little motivation for them to volunteer and fight to sustain the white-rule system. To many Rhodesian blacks, ZAPU and ZANU were not exactly the right answer. They represented hatred, communism and unbridled violence. For many more Rhodesian blacks, their lives in the rural tribal areas-politics aside-were increasingly interrupted by clashes and violence surrounding the issue of majority rule. To protest the atrocities of ZANU and ZAPU and protect their own livelihoods and tribal system, many black Africans voluntarily fought for white Rhodesia-in the RAR and in other elements of Rhodesian Security Forces.[12]

In fact, many more black recruits volunteered than could be accepted for service. One former RAR training officer stated that on recruiting days many more volunteers would stand outside the gates of the depot than required to fill 200 available training slots, from which about 130 trained soldiers would be selected and sent to the regiment after a six month training program.[13] This availability of volunteers did not substantially diminish throughout the Bush War, even after fighting intensified through the late 1970s and the RAR was constantly deployed to fight increasing numbers of ZANLA and ZIPRA. In an interview with Illustrated Life Rhodesia in 1975, Lieutenant Colonel David Heppenstall, commander of 1RAR, stated that the regiment had no shortage of candidates, "often 100 per cent more than we require, and sometimes more than that percentage. I can recall one occasion when we required 100 recruits, and 500 applied."[14]

The RAR soldiers were never forced to fight against their fellow tribesmen in the nationalist organizations. However, they chose to do so in great numbers. The rest of this chapter will explore the reasons why many black soldiers made this choice.

Income

In 1963, the lowest entry-level African soldier in the RAR was paid about 10 percent of what his "European," or white, counterpart made in the RLI. This pay system was inherited from the Federal Army of Rhodesia and Nyasaland, and before that, from the British colonial army. The unequal pay scale improved only very slightly, until major reforms were made in 1977-8 to increase pay and opportunities among black and white soldiers in the Rhodesian army. Even so, the relatively modest pay for an African recruit in the RAR was on par or better than most of his other options and placed the RAR soldier in rather good financial standing among his counterparts in the villages and farms of Rhodesia.[15]

Most other black Rhodesians were unskilled laborers in the commercial farms or mines, or lived in the tribal areas as subsistence farmers. With little education and slim opportunity for advancement outside the army or police, there were few opportunities elsewhere. Within the regiment, however, an RAR soldier could expect a solid starting pay and excellent chance for advancement from private to senior NCO in a merit-based promotion system.[16]

Stability

The RAR provided family housing, meals, education and medical care to its African soldiers and their families. When the soldier was in the field, his family received free meals, and they drew from the support network of other families of soldiers and officers on the military barracks. Unlike their white counterparts, black soldiers did not pay into a pension program, nor were they charged for meals themselves.[17] African terms of enlistment were 7 years, compared to 3 years for white enlistments, which provided a stable employment environment and ample opportunity for the RAR soldier to learn his craft and become proficient. The Rhodesian Army Education Corps ran schools for children and wives, as well as for the soldiers themselves, so there was substantial incentive for an RAR soldier to stay with the regiment once he had a family. This system also allowed children of RAR soldiers to grow up with an appreciation of the familial atmosphere of the regiment, which encouraged them to follow in the footsteps of their fathers.[18]

Family Pride

In selecting candidates for entry into the RAR, one of the easiest criteria to use was a family member's service and recommendation. The RAR recruited from all over Rhodesia, but most heavily from the Karanga, a tribe of the Shona people found predominantly in the Fort Victoria (now Masvingo) area in the central and southeastern part of the country. By recruiting heavily from one tribe, the regiment facilitated a family tradition among the Karanga, where grandfathers served in the Rhodesia Native Regiment during World War I, fathers served in the RAR in World War II, and sons counted the days until they too could stand the line as a *masodja* (soldier) like their forebears. By recruiting family members of RAR soldiers, the regiment gained known military skills from a ready pool of willing recruits.[19]

This is not to say the RAR was a Karanga tribal army. The demographics of the regiment were nearly identical to the black demographics of the nation. The RAR was about 85-90 percent Shona (not exclusively Karanga), 10-12 percent Ndebele, and a much smaller percentage of other tribes.[20] By comparison, the black Rhodesian population was approximately 19 percent Ndebele, 77 percent Shona, and 4 percent other tribes (Tonga, Venda, and Shangaan).[21]

Regimental Traditions

The RAR was originally established as a colonial rifle regiment of the British Army. As such, its regimental culture was defined by the same basic traditions and heritage as other regiments of the British Army, particularly other British colonial regiments in Africa such as the King's African Rifles and the Northern Rhodesia Regiment. To define this tradition and heritage, one must first understand how the British regimental system was applied in Africa.

In establishing security for its colonies, the British Empire relied heavily on locally recruited security forces to maintain order, put down riots and assist the police. By statute, the employment of British regular forces was restricted "to the defence of maritime fortresses and coaling stations."[22] The rest of the business of securing the empire was left to locally raised units under the control of civil authorities. This led to a dizzying array of colonial regiments loyal to the British Crown:

> From Wei-hai-Wei in North China to Port of Spain in Trinidad, and from Halifax in Nova Scotia to Hobart in Tasmania, there were soldiers organized, equipped and drilled in accordance with the manuals issued by the War Office in London. Some were called Scouts, others were named Levies, or Rifle Corps, or Guides, or Rangers, or Camel Corps, or Militias, or Military Police, or Defence or Frontier Forces. Seldom did their languages, organizations or roles exactly match and it was rare for the uniforms of any two to be precisely the same. But common to all, apart from the Drill Manual, was a dependence on the British Army to provide the officers and, in some cases, senior NCOs to command and train them in peace, and to lead them in war.[23]

The RAR was like any other colonial regiment, except in its lack of dependence on the British Army for its leadership. Because of its unique status as a self-governing colony after 1923, Southern Rhodesia recruited its own white officers into the RAR. Even the RAR's sister formations to the immediate north-the Northern Rhodesia Regiment and King's African Rifles-relied mainly on seconded officers and NCOs from the British Army, so the investment of RAR officers in fighting for their own regiment, for their own country, was quite a profound difference between the RAR and most other British colonial regiments.[24]

The colors and badge of the regiment, as mentioned in the previous chapter, represented the history and multicultural background of the regiment, respectively. The RAR took great pride in these symbols, as

British military tradition demands. Each regiment of the British Army designs and produces its own badge, and the RAR badge was no different. The badge and colors were unique to each regiment-the RLI also had its own badge, as did the BSAP and Rhodesia Regiment-and these were proudly displayed by the soldiers of the regiment on their uniforms and on parade.[25]

Parades were extremely important events for the RAR. The regiment conducted parades for many occasions: trooping the color, the Queen's birthday, reviews for distinguished visitors, Regimental Week (called Tanlwe Chaung, after the RAR's famous fight in Burma), and countless other occasions. Pride in appearance and smart drill were distinct points of pride for the RAR, and the men took great satisfaction in displaying the highest military standards on parade. The RAR seemed to enjoy this formal military culture a bit more than its sister infantry regiment, the RLI[26]-not to say that they looked better or drilled better, but that parades had more value as manifestations of military precision to RAR soldiers than to their RLI comrades. This formal tradition was a tremendous source of self-esteem for black Rhodesians, who had few other opportunities to work as peers with their white counterparts.[27]

Uniforms were also a source of pride for the men of the RAR, very much in the British colonial mold. African soldiers had a reputation of paying particular attention to detail and proudly wore their uniforms. Early in the war, the RAR soldiers turned out in immaculately starched khakis complete with putees around their ankles.[28]

The RAR bush hat was one item of uniform item that set the regiment apart. On the evolution of the distinctive RAR bush hat:

> In 1960, the commanding officer, Lieutenant-Colonel S. B. Comberbach, suggested that the RAR bush hat as worn by officers and warrant officers should be embellished in some way. The following year, a proposal was submitted to army HQ for the regiment to wear a three ostrich feather hackle in their bush hats. The commanding officer of 1KAR (Nyasaland) immediately objected, since his unit wore an ostrich feather hackle. The objection, of course, was upheld. One member of the Dress Committee then unkindly suggested that the RAR hackle should consist of Somabula bird feathers. The next sensible proposal, made by Major G. A. D. Rawlins, the battalion 2IC, was that the hackle should be made up of black ox-hair, the color worn by Lobengula's Mbizo Regiment whose former military kraal had

been near the present-day Methuen Barracks. This Matabele impi, which had retained a strong Zulu strain, had worn black trimmings on their arms and legs.[29]

In the pattern of the British regimental system, once an officer was badged into the RAR as his parent regiment, he stayed on the regimental rolls, and continued wearing his RAR uniform (badge, hat and dress uniform) no matter where he was assigned. This created a sense of belonging and ownership between the individual and his regiment. Very rarely did an officer change his parent regiment, and only then with the expressed approval of the Colonel of the Regiment.[30]

African Traditions and Practices of the RAR

In addition to these British traditions, the RAR had a few traditions and practices of its own. Its mascot, songs, and habit of secretly "naming" officers were all generated by the men and added to the RAR's culture and *esprit de corps*. Additionally, Platoon Warrant Officers (PWOs) were a unique duty position within the RAR, created to provide black supernumeraries and role models for the soldiers within the platoons. For example, RAR soldiers killed in action usually had two funerals-one for the regiment and one for their family in the *kraal*. All of these traditions served to cement the bond of loyalty between the African soldier and his regiment, and these bonds proved strong throughout the war.[31]

The regimental mascot, a goat, came about after some selection. Originally, the regiment had chosen a zebra as its mascot, but in practice found both the zebra and its successor, a donkey, unfit for military life. Finally, in May 1965, "Chief Cronje of the Fingo Tribe (a people who had accompanied Rhodes' Pioneer Column) solved the problem by presenting the regiment with a three-month old goat, promptly named 'Induna.'"[32] Induna rapidly became a favorite among the troops, and was trained to kneel on its forelegs and bow its head to "present arms." Induna lived to the age of eight, and on his death, was given a guard of honor, Last Post and Reveille, and was succeeded as the regimental mascot by another goat, Private Tendai.[33]

The soldiers had a habit of singing songs on route marches, details, at parties and anytime the opportunity presented itself. Accounts of the RAR songs marvel at the sound of the voice of the regiment, lifted in unison in "Sweet Banana," (the regimental song), or any other song relating to their experience in the war. It was quite common, particularly after some "lubrication of the throats" with a liberal dosage of *chibuku* (African home-brewed beer), for RAR soldiers to burst into boisterous song, mainly about their regiment and their history. These soldiers were extraordinarily happy, and justly proud of their achievements.[34]

African soldiers had a name for every officer in the regiment. It was a sign of acceptance for a white officer to be given a name by his soldiers, from Lt Col F.J. Wane (named *Msoro-we-gomo*, or "the top of the mountain"), who served with the Rhodesia Native Regiment in World War I and then rebuilt the RAR in 1940, to a young subaltern (named "Mr. Vice" after his father's position in the Rhodesian Air Force), or Captain (later Brigadier in the Australian Army) John Essex-Clark (named *Mopane*, after the tall, slender hardwood found in the Rhodesian bush). The names were not always particularly flattering or exalting, but the existence of a nickname demonstrated acceptance of an officer among the ranks of his soldiers, and were shared with the officers only occasionally by the NCOs of his platoon.[35]

Platoon Warrant Officers (PWOs) were a highly effective group of senior leaders in the RAR. These leaders were absolutely essential to sustaining and perpetuating the regimental culture of the RAR. PWO was a rank between Colour Sergeant and Warrant Officer. The PWO was the primary noncommissioned officer in a platoon. Most PWOs had at least 12-14 years of service, and they were responsible for ensuring that the orders of the platoon commander were carried out, caring for the soldiers, and training the members of the platoon-including the young lieutenant in command. If the platoon ever lost its lieutenant, the PWO was there to lead them in combat. The PWO was the principal instrument of regimental culture in the RAR. He knew, taught, and exemplified the history and values of the regiment. Without exception, every former officer interviewed spoke with special respect and reverence for this class of leaders in the regiment.[36]

The RAR truly fostered a familial environment among its soldiers and officers. When the regiment lost a soldier, for example, "the war stopped" for his platoon. As previously mentioned, his fellow soldiers held a funeral service at the regiment's chapel before releasing his body to his family in the *kraal,* where his relatives would gather for a days-long remembrance, drinking *chibuku* and singing. On rare occasions, families invited white officers from the regiment to these events, and the officers were honored to attend. Those officers who did attend tribal funerals recalled the events with great reverence as a profound experience.[37]

Leadership

The RAR was blessed during the course of its history with some outstanding leaders. Like other British colonial units in Africa, the officers were all white (until 1977, when the first black officers were commissioned), and most of the NCOs and all of the soldiers were black. By its nature, the RAR challenged a leader to adapt to cultural norms among his soldiers. Good officers in the RAR tended to be those who learned the languages and tribal customs of their soldiers, to understand what motivated them and what they feared.[38] Leading and training these soldiers took patience, as many of the problems presented by RAR soldiers-from multiple wives to witchcraft and spirit mediums-were completely foreign to white, "European" culture.[39]

Officers in the Rhodesian Army were very highly selected. In one typical officer intake in 1977, 650 candidates applied, 178 went to a selection board, and 45 were selected as officer cadets. Of these, 18 actually passed out of training as Second Lieutenants.[40] These 18 were then sent out to the Rhodesian Army based on where they were needed, and where their cadre saw that they fit best. According to a former officer cadet course instructor, "We paid great attention to the leaders we were going to use."[41] Officers who were to serve in the RAR were selected after completing the 13 month officer cadet course at the School of Infantry in Gwelo, after which, "we knew those guys [officer cadets] as well as their dads did."[42] In selecting which newly commissioned officers were sent to the RAR, the selection committee looked for the more serious, more outgoing officers, who were able to interact with people, and who instinctively led by example.[43]

Leadership by example was among the most important traits of an RAR officer. "If clean boots were the order of the day, the officer had to have the cleanest boots."[44] This was what the soldiers expected of their officers. RAR soldiers did not respond well to being given an order and expected to operate with initiative, as could well be done within the commando structure of the RLI. To function best, the RAR officer had to lead from the front, and they were selected and trained to do just that.[45]

Equally important was the leadership of the black noncommissioned officers and warrant officers. The Regimental Sergeants Major (RSMs), Company Sergeants Major (CSMs), Warrant Officers (WOs) and Platoon Warrant Officers (PWOs) were the epitome of what a black soldier could strive to be, until the first black officers were commissioned in July 1977.[46] These men knew, lived, and taught the history and traditions of the regiment to soldiers and officers alike, and they were among the most capable soldiers in Rhodesia.[47]

Leaders in the RAR understood the importance of morale. Napoleon's famous quote, "morale is to the physical as three is to one" was of utmost importance in training and leading African troops. "The aim was to create a unit with high morale; that is . . . the conquest of fear and the will to victory."[48] To that end, officers of the RAR ensured the basic needs of their soldiers-pay, family, education, pride-were met, and that their soldiers were constantly involved, never bored. In preserving morale over time, RAR leaders ensured the lessons and values of the regiment endured across generations and through the challenging situations the regiment faced.[49]

Conclusion

The reasons black soldiers joined the RAR are best summed up by CSM Obert Veremu, who said in 1975:

> I joined the Army when I was 20 years old, in 1953. My uncle is a soldier, and I knew if I joined the Army, I would be all right. I enjoy the work very much, and also it is very good to have everything free-uniforms, rations (our wives, too, get free rations while we are away on active service); medical attention, and schooling for our children. . . . These terrs are bad men. I have seen tribesmen who have been beaten to death by them. I also saw the woman whose lip they tore off with pliers. It is very bad what they are doing to their own people.[50]

In many respects, black Rhodesian soldiers enlisted for the same reasons most soldiers enlist in most armies-income, stability, pride, tradition, leadership. These pieces of regimental culture in the RAR are not virtues or characteristics that cannot be found anywhere else. The RAR is remarkable because these reasons and these bonds stayed true through the end of the war, through incredible pressure on black Rhodesians to succumb to the black nationalist groups and cast off a government that was portrayed to them as oppressive, racist and hateful.

The experience of the RAR in the Bush War provides an excellent opportunity to examine why soldiers choose to fight. During the course of the war, the atmosphere in which these soldiers worked was constantly changing and frought with racial, tribal, and international tension. The world in which the RAR soldier lived was turned upside-down, so that by 1980, his former enemy commander was his commander-in-chief. The enemy he had hunted down for 15 years, who had killed his friends, were integrated as peers into his formation. Militarily, the RAR was never defeated, but in the end, its war was lost. Loyalty for this soldier to anything but his regiment evaporated amidst the tremendous shifts resulting from the emergence of a majority-rule state of Zimbabwe.

Through to the end of the Bush War, and beyond, RAR soldiers remained loyal and steadfast to their regiment, and that must be their legacy. In the end, the values of the government-white-rule or otherwise-were irrelevant. It was the regiment that drew these men in, and their loyalty was more to their comrades and their heritage than to any particular government or cause.

Notes

1. CF20110920S0001, former RAR officer, interview; Nick Downie and Lord Richard Cecil, *Frontline Rhodesia*, DVD (Johannesburg: 30 Degrees South, 2007). In 1979, Prime Minister Muzorewa extended national service requirements to black Rhodesians. Prior to Muzorewa's governance, national service-that is, mandatory military service-only applied to whites. Throughout most of the Bush War, black service was strictly voluntary.

2. John Redfern, "Racial Discrimination in the Rhodesia and Nyasaland Army," Rhodesian Army memorandum, October 1962; John Redfern, "The Requirement for a Non-Racial Army in Southern Rhodesia," Rhodesian Army memorandum, October 1963. In 1962 and 1963, then-Captain (later Colonel) John Redfern at the Rhodesian Army School of Infantry wrote these two memoranda to the army commands of the Federal Army and Rhodesian Army respectively. In them, Redfern highlighted that racial practices of the Federal Army were unsuited for continued application, particularly in Southern Rhodesia. While his recommendations were not enacted at the time, it is noteworthy that the Rhodesian Army command concurred and forwarded them to the Rhodesian Air Force for action. The Air Force decided the *status quo* should remain, and the idea was not acted upon until 1977. The Rhodesian Army, and the RAR particularly, seemed far more open-much earlier-to racial integration than Rhodesian society as a whole (or American or British society at the time, for that matter). Additionally, during the course of researching this paper, the author personally interviewed over 30 Rhodesian Army veterans, from across the spectrum of service within the Rhodesian Security Forces (RSF). Without exception and in the most explicit terms, these men recounted their tremendous respect and admiration for the black soldiers with whom they had the privilege of serving. To say the African soldier was a respected member of a team is an understatement, as evident in how these men felt, and still feel, for their comrades.

3. Ronald Hyam, *Britain's Declining Empire: The Road to Declonisation 1918-1968* (New York: Cambridge University Press, 2006), 365; Eliakim M. Sibanda, *The Zimbabwe African People's Union: 1961-87* (Trenton: Africa World Press, 2005), 78. Sibanda is a professor in the history department at the University of Winnipeg, and a former ZAPU member.

4. Norma Kriger, *Zimbabwe's Guerilla War: Peasant Voices* (Cambridge: Cambridge University Press, 1993), 85. This quote is from ZANU's first policy statement under Ndabiningi Sithole.

5. Kriger, 82-85; Paul Moorcraft and Peter McLaughlin, *The Rhodesian War: A Military History* (Johannesburg: Jonathan Ball, 2009), 24-27. From January 1960 to the end of 1961, the number of independent nations in Africa went from 8 to 26, including Congo, Nigeria, Tanzania, Malawi, and Zambia. Algeria became independent in July 1962, and Uganda by that October. The "wind of change" was blowing south; this fact was readily apparent to Rhodesians.

6. Harold Macmillan (speech to South African Parliament, 3 February 1960).

7. Ian Douglas Smith, *The Great Betrayal: the Memoirs of Ian Douglas Smith* (London: Blake, 1997), 149-50.

8. CF20110920S0001, former RAR officer, interview.

9. Cecil John Rhodes (1853-1902) was the founder of Rhodesia and a self-avowed advocate of the British Empire. Arriving in Natal, South Africa in 1870, Rhodes quickly began to speculate in diamond claims in Kimberley. These mining interests formed the De Beers Consolidated Mines and gained Rhodes a fortune and considerable political power in the Cape Colony, which he devoted to the furtherance of his own world views and the greater spread of British influence across southern Africa and the globe. Rhodes' second will, written in 1877, bequeathed his yet unrealized fortune to found a secret society that would extend British rule over the whole world and colonize most parts of it with British settlers, leading, among other things, to the "ultimate recovery of the United States of America" by the British Empire. In 1890 (the same year his British South African Company pioneer column moved across the Limpopo River into Mashonaland to found Fort Salisbury and Rhodesia) Rhodes became premier of the Cape Colony, where he began arranging his vision of a South African federation under the British flag. After sponsoring a failed raid into the Transvaal under Leander Jameson in 1895, however, Rhodes was forced to resign this position. After falling from power, he devoted himself to building a railroad from the Cape to Cairo to solidify British influence on the African continent and facilitate the spread of the British Empire. Ultimately unsuccessful in this endeavor, Rhodes died in Muizenburg, South Africa in 1902, leaving most of his £6 million inheritance to Oxford University in the form of scholarships for students from the United States, the British colonies, and Germany. For more on Cecil John Rhodes, read one of his several biographies, such as *Cecil Rhodes: The Colossus of Southern Africa*, by J. G. Lockhart and the Hon. C. M. Woodhouse (New York: The Macmillan Company, 1963).

10. Smith, *The Great Betrayal*, 149-50.

11. CE20110909T0001, former RAR officer, interview. This former RAR officer recalled walking through a village near Fort Victoria late in the war to see nothing but old men, women and children. All of the military aged men were either in the RAR or in ZANLA. This effect on the population is often lost in military accounts of combat, but it had a tremendous effect on Rhodesian blacks. Neutrality was not an option.

12. Only the RLI and Special Air Service (SAS) remained all-white through the end of the war. Black soldiers were recruited and served in the RAR, British South African Police (BSAP), Selous Scouts, Rhodesia Regiment, Guard Force, and eventually the more controversial Security Force Auxiliaries.

13. CE20110908G0001, former RAR officer, interview by author, Johannesburg, Republic of South Africa, 8 September 2011. This officer recalled days when thousands of black Rhodesians stood outside the gates of Depot RAR to fill an advertised 200 open billets.

14. Beverley Whyte, "An Elite Group of Fighting Men," *A Pride of Men: The Story of Rhodesia's Army* (supplement to *Illustrated Life Rhodesia*), August 7, 1975: 16-19, 18.

15. Redfern, 1963, paragraph 6; James E. Dornan, ed., *Rhodesia Alone* (Washington, DC: Council on American Affairs, 1977), 36; The Internet Archive, "Employment and Climatological Data," http://www.archive.org/details/EmploymentAndClimatologicalData (accessed 21 November 2011); CE20110913M0001, former RAR officer, interview. The numbers to show salaries for military versus other occupations are difficult to find. However, interviews reveal that the RAR soldiers were generally better paid, with better opportunity for advancement, than their peers in other occupations. Redfern cites the African recruit's starting annual pay at £36.10.0 in 1963. According to 1973 data in Encyclopedia Rhodesia, 40 1/2 percent of black Rhodesians worked in agriculture and forestry (by far the leading occupation), which, according to a 1976 economic survey, paid Rh$125 per year, as of 1966. Converting between currencies, and accounting for inflation and the devaluation of the pound in 1972 precludes accurate analysis of these numbers. Interviews revealed, however, that African soldiers in the RAR had better opportunities in the regiment than in other occupations.

16. CE20110913M0001, former RAR officer, interview; CF20110920V0001, former RAR officer, interview by author, London, England, 20 September 2011.

17. Redfern, 1963, paragraph 11."European" soldiers were required to pay not less than 5 shillings per day for rations, and 7 ¼ percent of their income towards a pension plan. Africans did not pay for these benefits, although this accommodation by no means made up for the lack of pay and allowances for blacks.

18. Redfern, 1963, paragraph 11; CE20110913M0001, former RAR officer, interview; CF20110919H0001, former Rhodesian Army Education Corps officer, interview by author, Aylesford, England, 19 September 2011.

19. CE20110908M0001, former RAR officer, interview by author, Johannesburg, Republic of South Africa, 8 September 2011.

20. Binda, *Masodja*, 12; CE20110909R0001, former RAR officer, interview by author, Johannesburg, Republic of South Africa, 9 September 2011. In addition, these percentages are consistent with the regimental demographics given by most Rhodesian veterans interviewed for this project. By comparison, ZANU recruited predominantly from the KoreKore Shona, in the northeastern portion of the country, and ZAPU was almost entirely Ndebele and Kalanga, both tribes from Matabeleland.

21. Peter Moorcraft and Peter McLaughlin, *The Rhodesian War: A Military History* (Johannesburg: Jonathan Ball, 2009), 18.

22. James Lunt, *Imperial Sunset: Frontier Soldiering in the 20th Century* (London: Macdonald, 1981), 205.

23. Lunt, xiii.

24. CE20110908W0001, former RAR officer, interview by author, Johannesburg, Republic of South Africa, 8 September 2011; CE20110910H0001, former RAR officer, interview by author, Johannesburg, Republic of South Africa, 10 September 2011; CE20110908M0001, former RAR officer, interview. The British Army system of secondment allowed officers (and NCOs) to volunteer for service in colonial units, during which service they drew their regular pay plus pay from the colonial governments. In many British regiments, promotion or advancement often took a very long time, and service in regiments like the KAR or NRR frequently presented superb opportunities for better pay and more opportunity than continued service in regular British Army regiments. For more on how the secondment system worked in colonial regiments, read James Lunt's *Imperial Sunset*.

25. CE20110915B0001, former RAR officer, interview. This officer also stressed that the badge and uniform of the RAR was earned, not given to, the soldiers, and these were a source of great pride and individual accomplishment.

26. CE20110913M0001, former RAR officer, interview.

27. CE20110913M0001, former RAR officer, interview; Alexandre Binda, *The Saints: The Rhodesian Light Infantry* (Durban: 30 Degrees South, 2007), 75.

28. CE20110913M0001, former RAR officer, interview.

29. Binda, *Masodja*, 170.

30. CE20110913M0001, former RAR officer, interview.

31. CE20110908M0001, former RAR officer, interview.

32. Binda, *Masodja*, 173. In Sindebele, the language of the Ndebele, "InDuna" means "great leader."

33. Binda. In Chishona, the language of the Shona, "Tendai" is a female name meaning "thankful."

34. CE20110908M0001, former RAR officer, interview; CE20110915B0001, former RAR officer, interview. Most officers interviewed recall the songs and voices of the African soldiers in the RAR as a great motivator for all ranks.

35. Owen, 6; CE20110915B0001, former RAR officer, interview; Essex-Clark, 34. Owen describes Lt Col Wane's nickname; the young subaltern's came from an interview with the author, and Essex-Clark described his nickname.

36. CE20110908M0001, former RAR officer, interview; CE20110913B0001, former RAR officer, interview by author, Durban, Republic of South Africa, 13 September 2011; CE20110913R0001, former RAR officer, interview by author, Cape Town, Republic of South Africa, 13 September 2011.

37. CE20110908M0001, former RAR officer, interview; CE20110913M0001, former RAR officer, interview; CE20110915B0001, former RAR officer, interview.

38. CE20110908M0001, former RAR officer, interview; CE20110913B0001, former RAR officer, interview; CE20110913R0001, former RAR officer, interview.

39. Spirit mediums are a central piece of Shona culture. The Shona believe that all spirits are reincarnated after death, and that more powerful spirits continuously overlook the well-being of tribal areas and certain tribes. To the Shona, respect for the spirit medium is paramount. The 1893 Mashonaland uprising was led by two spirit mediums-Mbuya Nehanda and Kaguvi-both of whom were arrested and hung by the British South African Company. Before hanging, Nehanda promised that her bones would rise again to bring about a second uprising, or *Chimurenga,* which is what ZANU eventually claimed itself to be. Failure to understand the power of spirit mediums is a critical misstep for any foreign student of this culture. For more information on spirit mediums (which could easily fill a course of study on its own), see "The Social Organization of the Mashona, Part III," by C.J.K. Latham in the Rhodesia Native Affairs Annual 1979, http://www.archive.org/stream/TheRhodesiaNativeAffairsDept.AnnualFor1979/NADA2#page/n3/mode/1uu.

40. CF20110920V0001, former RAR officer, interview.

41. CE20110913M0001, former RAR officer, interview.

42. CE20110913M0001, former RAR officer, interview. Up to 1965, Rhodesian Army officer candidates went through the Royal Military Academy at Sandhurst. The cadet course at Gwelo stood up after UDI in 1965. It was modeled after Sandhurst, but tailored to Rhodesian Army requirements. One officer interviewed, a Sandhurst graduate, was charged specifically with establishing the cadet course at the Rhodesian Army School of Infantry after UDI.

43. CE20110913M0001, former RAR officer, interview.

44. CE20110913M0001, former RAR officer, interview.

45. CE20110913M0001, former RAR officer, interview; CE20110915B0001, former RAR officer, interview.

46. Binda, *Masodja,* 315. The first black officers were WO I Martin Nkatazo Tumbare and WO I Wurayayi Mutero, both former RSMs of 1RAR and 2RAR, respectively. They were commissioned in June 1977.

47. CE20110908M0001, former RAR officer, interview.

48. CE20110913M0001, former RAR officer, interview.

49. CE20110913M0001, former RAR officer, interview; CE20110908M0001, former RAR officer, interview; CE20110913B001, former RAR officer, interview by author.

50. Whyte, 18.

Chapter 3
Phase One: 1965-1972

The Rhodesian Bush War, fought between the white-rule Rhodesian government and the black nationalist organizations ZAPU and ZANU, effectively began on 11 November 1965, when Rhodesia unilaterally declared its independence from British rule. Initial incursions of nationalist groups into Rhodesia prior to UDI were small, sporadic, and generally disorganized. By August 1964 both ZANU and ZAPU[1] were banned from Rhodesia, and operated exclusively from Zambia. Small strikes and raids were their *modus operandi*.[2] The first real contact, in April 1966, occurred during Operation Pagoda, when several groups of ZANU insurgents infiltrated from Zambia to attack various targets, including infrastructure, police stations and white farms.[3] Subsequent insurgent operations during this phase did not substantially change from a pattern of small elements (10-30 insurgents) crossing the Zambezi River, living in the bush and striking targets of opportunity. Their aim was not really to incite a popular uprising, but more to cause instability in Rhodesia and force British military intervention to keep the peace. Throughout Phase One, insurgent leaders genuinely believed the British would intervene if they could stir up enough trouble. This type of sporadic contact continued until December 1972 when insurgent operators, realizing the British would not intervene and under the increasing influence of Maoist philosophy (particularly in ZANU), executed a significant change in tactics which opened the second phase of the Bush War.[4]

Rhodesian Army participation generally (and RAR participation specifically) in early contacts during Phase One was limited. Rhodesian police, principally the BSAP, saw terrorist incursions inside the borders of Rhodesia as criminal activities, falling exclusively under police purview. Once involved, the RAR found itself at the beginning of a learning curve in a new kind of conflict-unlike Burma, Malaya or Central African Federation deployments of recent memory. The regiment had much to learn as they faced their new enemies.

Operation Pagoda: The "Battle of Sinoia"

On the night of 1 April 1966, thirteen ZANU fighters crossed the Zambezi River from Zambia into Rhodesia. Seven additional fighters crossed the river the following night. These men were charged by ZANU leaders to begin the struggle to liberate Zimbabwe, in the hopes of securing funding from the Organization of African Unity (OAU), rallying black Rhodesians to the ZANU cause while inspiring whites to leave the country, and generally causing enough unrest inside Rhodesia for the British to deploy troops.[5] These twenty fighters were organized into four groups. The first group of five men, code named the *"Chimurenga"* group, were to go to the Umtali area in Eastern Rhodesia to attack the oil refinery and pipeline installations there. The second group, code named "Demolition" group, consisted of two men and was tasked to "blow up bridges and culverts along the road between Fort Victoria and Beitbridge."[6] The third group, code named *"Gukula-Honde,"* was made up of six men and was to "subvert locals in the Tribal Trust Lands south and west of Sinoia," then join the fourth group. This group, the "Armageddon" group, was the seven-man element that crossed the night of 2 April. Their mission was to train the locals subverted by the *Gukula-Honde* group, then raid farms and attack police stations.[7]

On 12 April, three members of the *Chimurenga* group spent the night in the *kraal*[8] of one of the members about forty miles from Umtali, while the other two stayed with a sympathizer at Old Umtali Mission. Locals reported the pair at Old Umtali to police, who apprehended them the following morning. After interrogation, these two led police to the *kraal* where the remaining three members were also arrested. Once this group was more thoroughly questioned, police learned of the existence of the other three groups and began to search for them.[9]

Meanwhile, Special Branch (SB)[10] also learned the location of the Armageddon group. During an Operations Coordinating Committee (OCC) meeting between the Rhodesian Army, Rhodesian Air Force (RhAF), BSAP and Central Intelligence Organization (CIO) to decide whether to eliminate this group or follow them in hopes of uncovering their contacts, Police Commissioner Frank Barfoot insisted in the interest of public safety that they could no longer remain at large. The resulting massive police operation, involving 83 BSAP policemen supported by four RhAF helicopters, took place near Sinoia on 28 April. Armed with World War One vintage Lee-Enfield .303 rifles[11] and no radios capable of communicating with the helicopters, the largely reservist police force surrounded the rendezvous point between the terrorists and the SB informant, and a firefight ensued. Despite poor communication and several tactical blunders during the operation, police killed all seven members of the Armageddon group, one from a helicopter-mounted MAG[12] after expending 147 rounds of ammunition.[13]

This operation was a major event for both sides. To ZANU, this was the start of the war in Rhodesia. In fact, 28 April-the day the Armageddon group met their fate-is a public holiday in Zimbabwe marking this beginning of the "*Chimurenga*," or "War of Liberation." As ZANU spokesman Washington Malinga said on 30 April 1966, it was "only the beginning." For the Rhodesian forces, this began a contest for jurisdiction over counterinsurgency operations between the army and the police. The Army absolutely insisted on its inclusion in any future counterinsurgency operations-they were better trained, better equipped and more experienced in hunting and dealing with insurgents (in Malaya and Federal deployments) than the police. The police, on the other hand, had a much more sophisticated intelligence network inside Rhodesia, constant contact with the population, and no desire to cede control within its own borders to the army. For their part, the RhAF helicopter crews recognized the need to have effective radio contact between the helicopters and ground units. Coming out of Sinoia, however, RhAF commanders began to resist future involvement of helicopters as gunships, seeing their role as exclusively support or troop transport.[14] All organizations recognized the need to train and prepare for future fights against ZAPU and ZANU in Rhodesia. While the RAR did not participate at Sinoia, the lessons learned there and passed across the Rhodesian Army directly contributed to future RAR experiences in the war.[15]

Operation Pagoda continued until 18 September 1966, resulting in the eventual death or capture of the remaining eight members of the Demolition and *Gukula-Honde* groups (as well as eleven ZAPU terrorists who infiltrated separately) by combined police and army operations involving small elements of both the RAR and RLI.[16] Perhaps the most important result of the experiences during Pagoda was the formation and use of Joint Operations Centres (JOCs), consisting of army, air force, BSAP and SB officers, plus any other relevant agencies specific to an operation. The JOC structure was more focused than the OCC, as its members were oriented locally, rather than nationally. This "command by committee" would remain a part of Rhodesian operations throughout the war, resulting in a more streamlined coordination process, improved communication and sharing of intelligence at the local, tactical level.[17]

The RAR participated in a few other operations in 1966. During these operations, the regiment further familiarized itself with JOC procedures, operations with the police, and methods of tracking and apprehending terrorists. The RAR's mastery of these concepts would become critically important in the coming years of operations against insurgents, particularly in Operation Nickel in 1967.[18]

Operation Nickel

On 10 August 1967, a policeman stopped an RAR patrol along the Wankie-Victoria Falls road in the northwest corner of the country to tell them he had found a pack in the area and he believed there were terrorists nearby. The platoon set out stop groups and initiated a sweep operation,[19] and quickly captured a terrorist. Interrogation would reveal this man to be a lost member of a 79-man combined ZAPU and South African African National Congress (SAANC) element that crossed the Zambezi and separated about four days previously. With one terrorist captured and a lead to many more, the RAR established a JOC at Wankie and brought in more police and soldiers. Operation Nickel was on, and it would prove one of the most formative experiences of the RAR in the Bush War.[20]

The ZAPU-SAANC group was divided into two subgroups. The first, code named *Lithuli*, was made up of 48 men (initially 54: 13 ZAPU and 41 SAANC),[21] and was to set up a base in the Tjolotjo area, near the Botswana border. The second group of 21 men (initially 23: 14 ZAPU and 9 SAANC) was code named *Lobengula*, and had Nkai as its objective, where it would receive assistance from members of the Zimbabwe Church of Orphans. From these two areas, each group was to establish recruiting and training bases to bring in local tribesmen, then attack European farms and police stations. After establishing these camps, the SAANC contingent would continue through Bechuanaland (Botswana) to the Sekhukuneland, Zululand and Transkei regions of South Africa.[22]

On 13 August, a BSAP patrol reported sighting insurgents near the Inyantue River area. Major Taffy Marchant, Officer Commanding (OC) A Company 1RAR, sent a seven-man section under the command of Captain Peter Hosking, his 2IC, along with two civilian trackers to follow up on this report. Marchant also sent a platoon led by Regimental Sergeant-Major (RSM) Aubrey Korb and Company Sergeant-Major (CSM) Timitaya shortly behind Hosking's detachment. Hosking made contact with what he believed to be a five-man terrorist element (it was actually the entire 21-man *Lobengula* group) and called for reinforcements. More police and more soldiers arrived by helicopter, and in the ensuing firefight both Hosking and Platoon Warrant Officer (PWO) Kephas were wounded, as well as police officers Tiffin and Phillips. Two RAR soldiers, Lance Corporal Davison and Private Korani, were killed in action. The RAR soldiers pulled back into an all round defense. The *Lobengula* group lost three killed and one seriously wounded (he would later be killed) in the contact.[23]

Over the next few days, Rhodesian and Botswana police arrested three members of the *Lobengula* group in separate incidents. The rest of the group was pursued by 3 Platoon, commanded by Lieutenant Ian Wardle, with 10 Platoon (under Lieutenant Graham Noble) and the Mortar Platoon (led by Lieutenant Piers) acting as stop groups. In another firefight, Wardle's platoon killed eight and captured six terrorists, completely accounting for the *Lobengula* group.[24]

Meanwhile, the 47-man *Lithuli* group, much more disciplined and better led (by a man named John Dube) than their counterparts, moved to the Leasha Pan, near the western section of the Tjolotjo Tribal Trust Land (TTL). On 19 August, the Mortar Platoon made contact with two members of this group, killing one of them. The platoon followed the tracks but lost contact. Dube assembled his men and quietly conducted two night movements into Tjolotjo TTL, while in the midst of security forces. By the morning of 22 August, the *Lithuli* group had established a camp in the Tjolotjo TTL, complete with camouflaged positions in an all round defense. Lt Nick Smith, commanding 1 Platoon, found tracks leading to this camp and followed them. At 1400, Smith's platoon made contact with the *Lithuli* group. In the firefight that followed, both Smith and PWO Timitaya were killed. Lance Corporal Mavaradze recounted:

> We then carried on firing, knowing the enemy was still there. Firing stopped again because we had no more ammunition and the enemy formed up with bayonets fixed. We withdrew, leaving our packs, radios, some rifles, and two dead bodies. After we had withdrawn we took up an all round defence and shared our remaining rounds. I then sent off three men to get help and later withdrew completely to the Wankie boundary road, and stayed there the night.[25]

The *Lithuli* group had suffered three killed, three wounded, and two lost to desertion. They enthusiastically took the abandoned equipment, food, and water and continued to move east. While moving, the group opened fire on a group of RAR soldiers, wounding one. "Hearing this firing, Lieutenant Peirson, commanding several ambush positions not far away, unwisely left his ambush position to investigate; tragically, he was mistaken for the enemy and shot and killed."[26]

On 23 August one of the deserters from *Lithuli* group was captured by 13 Platoon at Siwuwu Pools. Lieutenant Bill Winnall took 13 and 15 Platoons to pursue the lead resulting from his interrogation, and discovered tracks of approximately 30 men. Estimating himself to be about 3 hours behind the enemy, Winnall continued pursuit while the Mortar Platoon deployed in an ambush position on the Tegwani River. While waiting for an airstrike against the suspected enemy positions, Winnall decided to move his platoon into thick bush and establish a base for the night:

> No sentries were posted and no clearance patrols were sent out, the soldiers being scattered about the area in groups of two or three, smoking and chatting. Observing this carelessness, the enemy commander, Dube, seized the opportunity and, in company with one of his men, both wearing combat jackets (looted off 1 Platoon's dead) casually sauntered over to the security force position. Exchanging greetings with the AS [African Soldiers], Dube rapidly assessed the troops' deployment and then called out the order to his men to open fire.[27]

In the ensuing engagement, Lance Corporal Cosmos and Patrol Officer Thomas were killed, eight men were wounded (including Lt. Winnall), and the patrol withdrew to form a defensive position and evacuate the casualties.

At this point, the JOC accepted an RLI Commando[28] from Army Headquarters, in addition to 48 additional A Company soldiers and D Company 1RAR. These reinforcements arrived on 23 August, and immediately began patrolling in the vicinity of the Nata and Tegwani River junction, where Dube and his men were hiding. The JOC moved to Tjolotjo to better control security force actions.[29]

Dube then took seven men from the remnants of the *Lithuli* Group to find water and food. This small group got lost, and Dube was arrested in Botswana with three of his men on 28 August. When Dube failed to return to the main group, the remaining 31 men moved along the Tegwani on the night of 25 August. Without their leader, the group began to fall apart. Over the next two days, three more men deserted, the seventeen SAANC members split off to go to South Africa through Botswana, while the remaining eleven men, exhausted, stopped. On the morning of 28 August, two of these men deserted and were arrested. On 31 August, an insurgent named Ncube went to a *kraal* to get some food. While the old woman he had approached prepared his meal, she sent a girl to alert security forces, who promptly arrived and arrested Ncube. Ncube led 7 Troop, 1RLI with 11 Platoon, D Company 1RAR to the hide-out that he and five other insurgents occupied. In the ensuing firefight, four insurgents were killed and one fled.[30]

Through the next few days, security forces continued patrolling, looking for the rest of the *Lithuli* group. While following up on tracks leading away from a dead rhino, on 4 September, Lt. Noble and 10 Platoon engaged three more insurgents. One of the insurgents threw a grenade, killing Private Nyika and wounding Private Pezisayi. This set off a fire, which cooked off the enemy ammo and grenades and kept the remaining RAR soldiers at bay. Once the fire died out, 10 platoons swept the area and recovered three dead insurgents. Patrolling continued until Operation Nickel concluded the morning of 8 September 1967. In December, one of the outstanding insurgents was arrested in Plumtree, and in May 1968, South African police in Durban arrested another.[31]

The results of Operation Nickel were immediate and far-reaching. On the enemy side, ZAPU did not consider the operation a failure. Not only was the war now underway, but they had killed security forces and they were able to capitalize on their own version of the truth back in Zambia, where ZAPU was working to establish themselves as the better Zimbabwean movement to the OAU and their Zambian hosts. For their part, ZANU praised the courage of the fighters involved but condemned as a "gross blunder" the alliance with SAANC, whose efforts ZANU believed should have been focused in their own country, not in Rhodesia.[32]

For the RAR, the results were somewhat humbling. At the outset of the war, the Rhodesian Army expected the RAR to have no problems defeating the incompetent insurgents, due to its previous experience in Malaya and Federal deployments. But the regiment committed a few tactical blunders that hurt its reputation. The lessons learned for the RAR were the value of confident and decisive junior leadership (as Lt. Wardle and Capt. Hosking displayed), and the disastrous results of tactical carelessness, as seen in Lt. Winnall's actions. Also, during Nickel, RAR troops only carried 50 rounds of ammunition to limit the amount of weight each soldier had to carry. This practice came from the regiment's experience in Malaya and recent experience against ZANU and ZAPU, where their enemy did not stand and fight, and soldiers rarely had the opportunity to fire. RAR soldiers were also firing their newly issued FN FAL rifles on automatic, wasting the little ammunition they had. These faults were immediately corrected. Training subsequently focused on single, aimed shots, limiting the use of full automatic fire to lead scouts, and increasing the basic load for all RAR soldiers to 150 rounds.[33] Two ideas that were not immediately capitalized on, but would become crucial to success later in the war were the use of helicopters as fire support platforms (not just troop transport), and the importance of tracking-finding and following signs of enemy movement- to counterinsurgency operations.[34]

Perhaps of more strategic importance than these adjustments, however, was the subsequent offer of South African assistance to Rhodesia that came immediately after Nickel. The involvement of SAANC immediately brought the interest of the Pretoria government, eager to fight its own counterinsurgency away from home soil. Pretoria sent about 2,000 South African "police"[35] to assist Rhodesian Security Forces in COIN operations in the Zambezi valley. While Rhodesians considered their new South African allies to be clumsy, inefficient, and inexperienced-they were disparagingly called "ropes" (thick, hairy, and twisted) or "clumpies" (due to clumsy bushcraft)-for political reasons, they were welcome additions to the fight, and would eventually nearly equal the size of the Rhodesian regular army. South Africa would also add critical enablers such as helicopters and aircrews, along with tremendous economic assistance.[36] South African involvement in Rhodesia proved to be a "double-edged sword," however, as after the 1974 fall of Mozambique and Angola to communist guerrillas, South Africa became Rhodesia's only friend in the global community. South African Prime Minister John Vorster would use to his advantage later in the war.[37]

Operation Cauldron

The RAR was deployed several more times through the first phase of the war, pursuing groups of terrorists across sparsely populated areas of the country, in constant cooperation with the police and with the willing assistance of the locals. In March 1968, a game ranger came across a wide track made by terrorists conveying supplies between several camps they had established near the Chewore River. He called in the police, and Operation Cauldron began, which was to be a "baptism of fire" for the RAR's sister regiment, the RLI. The RLI would emerge from Cauldron as a tested, proven and capable unit, earning the nickname, "The Incredibles," which would stick through the end of the war.[38]

The enemy in Operation Cauldron was once again a mixture of ZAPU and SAANC, a contingent of 100-125 men whose aim was to establish a number of base camps between the Zambezi River and Sipolilo in the north-central part of the country. From here, locals were to be trained and armed, and eventually unleashed on an unsuspecting Rhodesia at a later date. The RLI, with the SAS and limited participation from the RAR, put an end to those plans in the ensuing months, killing 58 terrorists and capturing a large number, while the rest limped back to Zambia.[39]

The RAR participation in Operation Cauldron consisted of 14 Platoon, E Company 1RAR, led by Lieutenant Ron Marillier. Although Marillier was awarded the Bronze Cross of Rhodesia for his actions during Cauldron, his platoon-and the RAR-drew heavy criticism from the RLI and Army command (including Colonel Peter Walls, later the Rhodesian Army Commander) for multiple failures in the face of the enemy. Essentially, the RAR soldiers proved reluctant to move under fire and attack the enemy. Several attempts to rally these soldiers proved unsuccessful, and in their first contact, the RAR platoon and the RLI commando moving with them were forced to pull back and call in an airstrike against the enemy position. The RAR lost one soldier, Corporal Erisha, killed and two wounded, PWO Herod[40] and Private Wilson. Marillier had only taken command of his platoon the day before it was moved into Operation Cauldron, so he did not know the names of most of his men, nor did they know him. In contact, the men would not follow him, and control of the platoon broke down. These shortfalls can be attributed to the elevated sense of enemy capability amongst RAR soldiers coming out of Operation Nickel, and the fact that the RAR was still adjusting to its new war, discovering that their experience in Malaya and Nyasaland did not exactly apply against ZAPU and ZANU. Fortunately, both of these factors would evaporate rapidly in the coming operations, and the RAR was to become quite proficient at hunting and killing insurgents in the Bush War.[41]

Operation Cauldron had a few significant outcomes. For its small part in the operation, the RAR learned more about how to fight its new enemy. Lessons from Cauldron, combined with Nickel, would be applied in future operations to bring the RAR back into the fold as a top-tier counterinsurgent force. Also, the RLI proved itself as an effective force, beginning its own sterling reputation. Unfortunately, a third outcome was that the Rhodesian Army-indeed the entire Rhodesian population-began to believe that the military situation was well in hand, and this war would not be a major problem. This was much to their detriment, as the years from 1968-72 are marked by an astonishing lack of pursuit, adjustment, and analysis by Rhodesian Security Forces against their enemy. The enemy, meanwhile, were adjusting their tactics.[42]

Conclusion

The RAR began the Rhodesian Bush War as respected veterans of Burma, Malaya, and Central African Federation deployments-by far the senior regiment of the Rhodesian Army, expected to outperform its peers and emerge victorious from every fight. In its first two operations against ZAPU and SAANC, however, the regiment displayed some disturbing tactical blunders. The upstart RLI (only formed in 1961), however, came into its own during Operation Cauldron-in the face of a questionable RAR performance.

Between Nickel and Cauldron, the RAR proved that seniority did not instill competence, and that adjustments were required to succeed in this new war on Rhodesian soil. The Commanding Officer, Lieutenant Colonel Bill Godwin, recognized this need and immediately set out to make these corrections, and regain the vaunted reputation of the regiment. Valuable lessons learned by the regiment in these first operations-the value of tracking and moving small units around the battlefield, the price of overestimating the enemy (as Marillier's platoon did during Cauldron), and the necessity of competent, effective junior leaders-would lead to phenomenal success later in the war. Ironically, most of these shortcomings for the RAR were also lessons learned from Malaya, although some early accusations against the RAR concluded that its "Malayan Way" nearly caused failure in Operation Nickel.[43]

In 1972, several key events occurred which changed the face of the war. ZANU, under the influence and mentorship of Maoist Chinese advisors, realized that success in their protracted war depended on the support of the population, and their tactics shifted to coercion and collusion with rural villagers in Rhodesia. ZAPU followed suit, although much more slowly, and both groups increased their operational tempo. The regiment was about to get very busy.[44]

Notes

1. Originally banned in 1961, ZAPU continued to operate outside Rhodesia as "ZAPU" and inside Rhodesia as the People's Caretaker Council (PCC). In 1964, the PCC was also banned, along with ZANU.

2. Kriger, 88.

3. Moorcraft, 29; Binda, *Masodja*, 204-5.

4. Wood, *Counterstrike*, 37. Historian Richard Wood's five phases of the Rhodesian Bush War as outlined in *Counterstrike* will frame this paper's discussion of how the RAR adapted and changed through the war. Phase 2 began with the 1972 Altena Farms attack and ended with the 1974 Portuguese withdrawal from Mozambique, which opened the northeastern border area to ZANLA incursions, substantially increasing the number and frequency of contacts between RSF and CT forces that characterized Phase 3 (1974-1977). Phase 4 (1977-April 1979) saw massive concessions by the Rhodesian government towards majority rule, ending in the 1979 election of a black Prime Minister, Bishop Muzorewa. Phase 5 (April 1979-April 1980) was characterized by increasing international pressure, failure of outside states to recognize Muzorewa's government, and the election of Robert Mugabe as president of Zimbabwe which ended the Bush War.

5. Wood, *Counterstrike*, 75; Binda, *Masodja*, 204-5; Moorcraft, 29-31. Moorcraft and McLaughlin's account of Sinoia varies slightly in accounting for the number and nature of the ZANU groups. They broke the Pagoda / Sinoia groups into 21 terrorists split into 3 groups. As Wood and Binda wrote much later after the war (*The Rhodesian War* was originally written in 1982), both had access to actual operational reports and other primary sources, so where numbers or dates disagree, Wood and Binda's data are used throughout this paper, as cited here.

6. Binda, *Masodja*, 204-5.

7. Binda.

8. *Kraal* is an Afrikaans corruption of the Portuguese *curral*, meaning cattle pen or enclosure. In Rhodesia, this word described an African village or dwelling.

9. Binda, *Masodja*, 204-5.

10. Special Branch of the Central Intelligence Organization provided much of the intelligence throughout the war. This organization had an extensive network of informers and operatives in the tribal areas and outside Rhodesia who reported to CIO and to the police. Integration of Special Branch intelligence with military operations was slow to evolve, and caused quite a bit of frustration within the army early in the war.

11. Wood, *Counterstrike*, 77. The Armageddon group, like the other ZANU terrorists sent into Rhodesia, was armed with a mixture of semi-automatic

"Soviet SKS 7.62mm rifles, French MAT-49 9mm submachine guns, German Luger 9mm pistols, Soviet F1 and RGD5 grenades," placing them at a distinct firepower advantage over the much older BSAP bolt-action Lee-Enfields.

12. *Mitrailleuse d'Appui Général*, or General Purpose Machine Gun, designed by the Belgian company *Fabrique Nationale* (FN), was the standard issue machine gun used by the Rhodesian Army. It is an automatic, air-cooled, gas-operated machine gun firing belt-fed 7.62×51mm NATO ammunition from an open bolt. While it was experimentally mounted in helicopters, as noted here, it was far more prevalent among ground troops, issued at one per infantry rifle section (8-10 men), and later fireforce stick (4 man element), in the RAR and RLI. This machine gun was also adopted for use by the US Army and US Marine Corps in the mid-1980s as the M240. Rhodesian helicopters would later use twin Browning .303 machine guns and, eventually, 20mm cannons as armament.

13. Wood, *Counterstrike*, 76-79; Binda, *Masodja*, 204-5; Moorcraft, 31; Ron Reid-Daly, "The War in Rhodesia" in *Challenge: Southern Africa within the African Revolutionary Context,* ed. A. J. Ventner (Gibraltar: Ashanti, 1989), 149.

14. Reid-Daly, *Challenge*, 156; Binda, *Masodja*, 224; Wood, *Counterstrike*, 61-63. Until 1973, RAF use of helicopters as gunships was largely experimental, and RhAF command continued insisted on using helicopters in a support, rather than combat role. This position would later be reversed at the army's insistence, RhAF Alouette helicopters equipped with MAGs, twin .303 Browning machine guns with reflexive sights, and by July 1974 with French Matra MG151 20mm cannons, were employed as "K-Cars" in fireforce operations with great effect.

15. Moorcraft, 29; Wood, *Counterstrike*, 80; Reid-Daly, 149-50; Binda, *Masodja*, 205.

16. Binda, *Masodja*, 206-10.

17. Wood, *Counterstrike*, 80.

18. Binda, *Masodja*, 206-7. Operations Grampus and Vermin are two such operations mentioned by name in the Regimental History. The JOC quickly became the central node of information, and its maturing process as a command element became evident as operations continued.

19. Rhodesian Army, COIN Manual, Part II-ATOPS [Anti-Terrorist Operations] (Salisbury, 1975), 91-2. Rhodesian tactics frequently called for sweep operations using "stop groups" and "sweep groups." Typically, stop groups-the hunters-were placed in concealed positions along likely avenues of escape, crossing points or natural lines of drift. The sweep group-the hounds-then deliberately searched the entire area to flush the target out of hiding and into a waiting ambush at the stop group position. This tactic, refined and employed from helicopters, was the basis for fireforce, and it was employed throughout the war.

20. Binda, *Masodja*, 214.

21. Binda, *Masodja*, 215. After crossing the Zambezi, 10 men were separated from the two groups, one of whom was captured by security forces. 2 additional men of mixed race "were tasked with a separate mission in South Africa," bringing the initial total to 79, with 69 remaining when the RAR made contact."

22. Binda.

23. Binda, *Masodja*, 215-6.

24. Binda.

25. Binda, *Masodja*, 218-9.

26. Binda, 219.

27. Binda.

28. Binda, *Saints*, 46. In 1965, the RLI restructured from a conventional infantry battalion into a "commando" battalion. While keeping its designation as a battalion, its subordinate units were called commandos rather than companies, and troops rather than platoons. The RLI had four commandos (numbered 1, 2, 3, and Support). Each commando was further subdivided into five troops of 25 men (as opposed to three platoons of 37 men), although they typically operated at strength of four troops due to manpower shortages and casualty rates. So, an RLI commando consisted of 100-125 men divided into 4-5 troops.

29. Binda, *Masodja*, 219-20; Binda, *Saints*, 60.

30. Binda.

31. Binda.

32. Binda, *Saints*, 64; Moorcraft, 32-3.

33. Binda, *Masodja*, 224; CE20110910H0001, former RAR officer, interview; CF20110920H0001, former RAR officer, interview by author, London, England, 20 September 2011.

34. Reid-Daly, *Challenge*, 156.

35. This number also included army and air force units, but the word "police" was used to obscure South African military involvement in what was internationally viewed as a British affair.

36. Moorcraft, 32; Reid-Daly, *Challenge*, 158-9.

37. Wood, *Counterstrike*, 53.

38. Binda, *Saints*, 64.

39. Binda, *Masodja*, 227.

40. Binda, *Saints*, 78. PWO Herod, while recovering from his wounds, was credited with saying famously to RLI Sgt Tim Baker, "We of the RAR used to laugh at your soldiers. To us they looked like boys. But they showed us how to fight. They have the faces of boys, but they fight like lions."

41. CE20110910H0001, former RAR officer, interview; Reid-Daly, *Challenge*, 161-2; Binda, *Masodja*, 227.

42. Moorcraft, 33; Binda, *The Saints*, 77-8; Binda, *Masodja*, 227.

43. Reid-Daly, *Challenge*, 155; CE20110912G0001, former RAR officer, interview by author, Durban, Republic of South Africa, 12 September 2011.

44. Wood, *Counterstrike*, 35-37.

Chapter 4
Phase Two: 1972-1974

The problem of establishment of bases is of particular importance. This is so because this war is a cruel and protracted struggle . . . [S]ome part of our country-or, indeed, most of it-may . . . be captured by the enemy and become his rear area. It is our task to develop intensive guerrilla warfare over this vast area and convert the enemy's rear into an additional front. Thus the enemy will never be able to stop fighting. In order to subdue the occupied territory, the enemy will have to become increasingly severe and oppressive.

— Mau Tse-Tung, *On Guerrilla Warfare*

From 1971 and leading to the December 1972 attack on Altena Farm in northeast Rhodesia, ZANU adopted a Maoist strategy to establish a base area in Rhodesia, spread security forces thin and collapse morale through consistent attacks on rural targets. In response, Rhodesian forces established a JOC at Centenary. This JOC became the headquarters for Operation Hurricane across the northeast portion of Rhodesia, and the first of six operational areas (Hurricane, Thrasher, Repulse, Tangent, Grapple, and Splinter) that would define the Rhodesian war effort.[1]

This period saw several security force developments, including the establishment of the first Operational Area (Hurricane); the start of the Protected Village (PV) program in contested areas of the country; the inception of the Selous Scouts; and the early development of a rapid airborne reaction force, called Fireforce, to quickly strike on actionable intelligence.[2]

Politically during this phase, the December 1971 rejection of the Home-Smith agreement for transition to majority rule stymied an early Rhodesian political solution to the growing insurgency and contributed to turmoil within and outside of Rhodesia. The Portuguese withdrawal from neighboring Mozambique in 1974, and subsequent handover of Mozambique governance to the *Frente de Libertaçao de Moçambique* (FRELIMO) guerrillas, effectively eliminated the Rhodesian government's crucial eastern ally. This left Rhodesia's sole remaining friendly ports and borders with South Africa. FRELIMO would also provide sanctuaries in Mozambique for ZANLA and open the north and east border regions to ZANLA infiltrations unencumbered by the more restrictive terrain of the Zambezi River along the Zambian border. Despite these developments, by

1974 security forces had reduced the number of insurgents in the country to 60 individuals, all contained in the northeast.³

The Home-Smith Agreement and Pearce Commission

To understand the environment in which the RAR operated during this phase of the war, it is important to understand the significant political events that occurred. As the RAR began to consistently engage and pursue their enemy, much was in turmoil in Rhodesia.

In September 1965, the British Commonwealth Relations Office (CRO) established five principles for Rhodesian independence:

> First, the principle and intention of unimpeded progress to majority rule, already enshrined in the 1961 constitution, would have to be maintained and guaranteed. There would also have to be guarantees against retrogressive amendment of the constitution. There would have to be immediate improvement in the political status of the African population. There would have to be progress towards the ending of racial discrimination. The British Government would need to be satisfied that any basis proposed for independence was acceptable to the people of Rhodesia as a whole.⁴

A sixth principle was added in January 1966: no oppression of the majority by the minority, or of the minority by the majority.⁵

The first principle-unimpeded progress to majority rule-was the nominal reason Britain refused to grant independence to Rhodesia.⁶ Under the 1961 constitution, which was referenced by the CRO above and annexed to the UDI seven weeks later, there were two voter rolls—"A" roll and "B" roll. While these rolls were not explicitly racially divided, the A roll was restricted to higher thresholds of property, education and income-thus, higher contributions to income tax revenues-and was predominantly white. The B roll, with lower standards, was almost entirely black.⁷

The 65 seats of the Rhodesian Assembly were subdivided into 50 constituency and 15 district seats. Both rolls voted for constituency and district seats. However, the 1961 constitution had a "cross-voting" influence built in: that is, B roll votes were capped at 20 percent of the total vote for the 50 constituency seats, and A roll votes were likewise capped at 20 percent for the 15 district seats. The end result of this complicated voting system was that whites (A roll voters) had a controlling majority of 50 constituency assembly seats, while the black majority only effectively controlled 15 district seats. This breakdown was representative of contributions to "the fisc," or the income tax revenue of Rhodesia, but it was grossly out of step with the demographics of the country. In asking black leaders to accept this constitution, the Rhodesian government was effectively asking that they accept a long, slow road to majority rule: once enough blacks met the education, property and income requirements to qualify as A roll voters, they would gain parity in electing the constituency seats. Black nationalist leaders initially signed an agreement endorsing this constitution, but later reneged and urged the black population to reject the constitution during the 1962 referendum.[8]

In 1969, the Rhodesian Front proposed a new constitution, which declared Rhodesia to be a republic.[9] This UDI constitution still offered a viable path to majority rule, thus meeting the first principle laid out by the CRO, but it was an even slower path than the 1961 constitution. Smith and the Rhodesian Front still believed they had made generous concessions toward majority rule, and had met the first four principles outlined by the CRO.[10] As a step backward on the path to majority rule, however, the UDI constitution alienated more of the moderate black population from the Rhodesian Front and provided a rich opportunity for ZANU and ZAPU to capitalize on the Rhodesian Front's apparent unwillingness to share power.

In the April 1970 general election, the Rhodesian Front won all 50 A roll seats. In April 1971 the newly appointed Conservative British Foreign Secretary, Lord Alec Douglas-Home, flew to Salisbury to discuss the new Rhodesian constitution and assess the acceptability of this document as meeting the principles for British recognition of Rhodesia. From April to November 1971, Douglas-Home negotiated with Smith's representatives to create a compromise agreement. When Douglas-Home left for England in November, he assured Smith that London would be satisfied, pending a few formalities. The resulting agreement conceded additional B roll seats in the Rhodesian Assembly-giving black voters a total of 22 seats (still short, however, of a "blocking third" to prevent additional amendments to the constitution). In the compromise Home-Smith Agreement:

> Rhodesia had to declare its intention to make progress toward ending racial discrimination; accept a new declaration guaranteeing individual rights and freedoms; include steps to enable more Africans to compete on equal terms with whites for civil-service jobs; review the cases of all detainees and restricted persons; and set up an independent committee to study racial discrimination and make recommendations to the Rhodesian government. Up to £50 million in British aid was to be given to Rhodesia over a ten-year period, and the Rhodesian government was to match this sum to promote educational and job opportunities for Africans.[11]

This agreement was accepted by both the Rhodesian Front and the British representatives as meeting the first four principles laid out by the CRO in 1965.[12]

To meet the fifth principle-satisfaction of the British Government that the proposal was acceptable to the people of Rhodesia as a whole-the British formed a twenty-one man commission, chaired by a British judge, Lord Edward Holroyd Pearce. Pearce's three deputy chairmen were Sir Maurice Dorman (former Governor-General of Sierra Leone and Malta), Sir Glyn Jones (former Governor of Nyasaland), and Lord Harlech (former British Ambassador to the United States). Neither Pearce nor Harlech had any experience in Africa, and while all of the other commissioners were former colonial officers in Africa, none of the commissioners were black, which instantly eroded any credibility of the commission amongst black nationalist leaders.[13]

The Pearce Commission arrived in Rhodesia in January of 1972 and began meeting with Rhodesians to determine their views on the Home-Smith Agreement (also called the Anglo-Rhodesian Agreement). From January to March, the commission met with about 6 percent of the black population amid violence between police and African National Council (ANC)[14] nationalists against accepting the agreement. In May, Pearce reported to Lord Douglas-Home and Parliament that black Rhodesians "roundly rejected" the Home-Smith Agreement and that British sanctions should continue.[15]

According to Ian Smith, the Pearce Commission's report was a fraud, because apart from the fact that "the vast majority of our black people were unable to comprehend what was taking place, the commission had seen less than 5 per cent of our black people-and yet they were prepared to submit a report purporting to represent the views of 100 per cent!"[16] However, according to Dr. Wellington Nyangoni, a former ZANU member and African history professor at Brandeis University, "African opposition to the Anglo-Rhodesian Agreement was overwhelming, and their rejection of the Agreement rendered it unacceptable."[17] Whatever the cause for the Pearce Commission's findings, by 1971 it was clear that Rhodesia was beginning to fragment along racial lines, either at the urging of black nationalists of the ANC, ZAPU, and ZANU or because of an out-of-touch Rhodesian Front government.

Amidst all of this turmoil, the RAR continued to recruit, fight and thrive as a multicultural organization. None of the political or social dynamics in motion within the country were reflected within the regiment. The controversy surrounding the Home-Smith Agreement and the Pearce Commission did not affect the availability of black recruits for the RAR at all, nor did it seem to affect soldiers serving in the regiment. Indeed, the regiment still had many more recruits than it could accept waiting outside its gates on recruiting days, and the soldiers serving in the regiment saw themselves as a staunchly apolitical force, undeterred by the political events surrounding them. Like most other RAR traditions, the absence of politics in the regiment was a British Army notion not copied in ZIPRA, ZANLA, or later in the Security Force Auxiliaries.[18]

Operation Hurricane

In December 1972, ZANU insurgents attacked Altena Farm near Centenary "to study the reaction of the enemy and his tactics so we could decide upon our own tactics,"[19] according to their commander, Rex Nhongo. ZANLA attacked from Chiweshe TTL, where they had established a base. The farm was randomly selected as a target, but the attack deliberately provoked a Rhodesian response, which ZANLA watched very carefully. ZANLA operators had been in the Chiweshe TTL for over a year, and had subverted the population in much of the Northeast portion of the country. Their intent was not only to subvert the population but to force RSF to spread themselves out, resulting in constant attrition of troops and morale over time. ZANLA insurgents had given up on the idea that the British Army would intervene on their behalf if they could generate enough civil unrest. They were learning from their Chinese mentors, and their strategy and tactics shifted to a more popular struggle, focused on setting conditions for insurgency among the *kraals* and tribal areas. Only once conditions were set among the population would ZANLA conduct any sort of military action, carefully avoiding costly direct confrontation with security forces, where ZANLA was at a disadvantage.[20]

The Rhodesian response to the attack on Altena Farm was to establish a JOC at Centenary and initiate Operation Hurricane to find and destroy the ZANLA forces in the area. To that end, a mixture Rhodesian Security Forces (RSF), including elements of 1RAR, were deployed into the operational area as the first troops in what would be an eight-year operation. These troops immediately noticed that the locals were no longer as willing to cooperate with security forces-they were afraid of ZANLA reprisals, and their chief was a ZANLA supporter.[21]

Until Operation Hurricane, Rhodesian Security Forces believed they had the situation well in hand. They believed that black Rhodesians would fully support the white government's efforts against the insurgents, and that no major adjustments to their tactics were necessary, despite reports to the contrary (including documents captured during an SAS raid against a FRELIMO-ZANLA[22] base camp in Mozambique). It took the attack on Altena Farm to sound the alarm within the Rhodesian command. Once Rhodesian commanders realized that the paradigm of universal black support was an illusion, they made several adjustments in how they fought the war as well. The RAR would play a vital role in implementing these tactics.[23]

Protected Villages

One of the adjustments made by RSF was an effort to isolate the population from insurgent influence and create "no-go" areas[24] in sparsely populated regions by creating Protected Villages (PVs). The effectiveness of these villages was mixed-they did help create civilian "no-go" areas to facilitate RSF pursuit of insurgents, but they failed to address the core issue of popular support for the insurgency.[25]

PVs were not new to the RAR soldiers, some of whom had experience in Malaya, as well as in Mozambique with Portuguese troops.[26] Malayan PVs-called "New Villages"-were highly effective at denying insurgent access to the population. The Portuguese versions of PVs, called *aldeamentos*, were not as effective because the Portuguese program in Mozambique was hastily executed and inadequately resourced.[27] The Rhodesian PVs were a blend of the Malayan and Portuguese concepts, and were a strategic failure of the Bush War.

According to counterinsurgency theorist Sir Robert Thompson, there are three main objectives of a PV strategy:

> The first, a prerequisite for the other two, is the protection of the population. . . . The most vital aspect of protection, however is the elimination within the hamlet of the insurgent underground organization. Until this is done, no hamlet will be secure against repenetration and treachery, nor can the people themselves be expected to take positive action on behalf of the government until insurgent agents and supporters within the hamlet have been removed. The second object . . . is to unite the people and involve them in positive action on the side of the government. . . . This can only be done by involving the people in a small way in national policies which both affect and benefit them, first in the defence of their community and secondly in its development. The third objective . . . is this development in the social, economic, and political fields. . . . The significant point here is that at the end of

the [Malayan] Emergency very few families wished to leave their new homes and return to their old sites.[28]

In practice, Rhodesian PVs did not separate the population from insurgent influence prior to moving them into the villages, nor was there ever enough investment in the infrastructure, social, economic or political fields to influence the population to support the government.[29]

In establishing the PV program, Rhodesian Deputy Minister of Law and Order Wickus de Kock emphasized that the purpose of the program was to create no-go areas, where access was restricted to "authorised members of the Security Forces."[30] This is a very different emphasis from the Malayan model, which focused on isolating the population from insurgents by first focusing on meeting security and infrastructure needs of the villagers themselves. In contrast to de Kock's policy, the Rhodesian Army stated that the intent of the operation that relocated people into PVs was "to deprive terrorists of their vital contact with the civilian population, particularly at night, when they force tribesmen to accommodate and feed them as they move through the area."[31] These two shades on the intent of the PV program reveal a rift between government policy and army practice, and neither of the stated intents addressed what was most successful in Malaya- safeguarding and improving conditions for the people.[32]

A third perspective on the intent of PVs came from an Internal Affairs planning document, which stated, "The short term objective is the removal of the African people from terrorist influence for the sake of national security, but the full attainment of this short term aim must surely result in our reaching the ultimate goal of more concentrated and more rapid development of the African people and the areas which they inhabit."[33] The emphasis of the PV program never shifted to that second long term goal of development due to lack of resources, poor planning and misunderstanding amongst planners of the intent of the program.[34]

The result of this confused PV policy was the hasty establishment of poorly planned, insufficiently secured and under-resourced villages that inspired no confidence in the government and were still vulnerable to insurgent attacks. The civilians' situation had most certainly not improved, and in their view it had deteriorated. According to a black Member of Parliament, Aaron Mungate, the main objections to PVs among the black population were:

1. The only people who were protected were those within the keep itself (i.e. the guards).

2. In the majority of the Protected Villages no timely and adequate water supply had been installed.

3. People had been forced from their traditional, and in some instances, substantial homes with no compensation and no aid towards buying materials to erect new ones.

4. Because only the gates of the Protected Villages were guarded, the fences around the village did not prevent communication between the villagers and the insurgents.[35]

The Rhodesian PV program suffered from two main shortcomings in execution. First, there was "an over-emphasis on the short term goal of physically concentrating the local population and the freedom of action this would give the Security Forces. Second, the program never had the resources committed to it-either financially or militarily, to succeed.[36] In the only truly successful example of population control the Rhodesians had (Malaya), the government committed adequate economic resources to the endeavor, resulting in New Villages truly becoming better places to live than their alternative. This was a lesson that the British had learned rather painfully by the time the RAR were deployed there in 1956. In Malaya, there were also more than enough security forces to isolate the villages from the insurgents-Rhodesia had neither the will nor the manpower to commit to PV security early enough to make a difference. Instead, PVs became unsanitary breeding grounds for contempt toward the government, and excellent targets for coercion and manipulation by the insurgents.[37]

The PV program is one area where the RAR could have played a tremendous role in turning popular support back to the government of Rhodesia. Had the Rhodesian government invested the time and effort into developing meaningful local protection of the PVs at their inception-possibly using RAR platoons as partners and trainers for village security forces, at least the security situation within PVs would have improved, and potential inclusion of the villagers in securing their own fate may have prevented their availability to the insurgents for psychological and physical attacks. Eventually, two security initiatives would attempt to redress the vulnerability of PVs and the surrounding tribal areas-Guard Force and Security Force Auxiliaries (*Pfomu re Vanhu*, mentioned earlier). Both initiatives were severely challenged in providing adequate training, equipment, and supervision. By the time these forces were stood up, they couldn't be trained fast enough to meet the threat.[38]

The RAR knew how to train African soldiers. They had established a rigorous selection and training program of their own, and understood quite well how to overcome the challenge of taking a raw recruit from a Rhodesian *kraal*, with very limited education, no experience with a rifle, and little cultural understanding of how the army was structured and turning him into a capable soldier-loyal and dedicated to his regiment. The development of such a force took time, as the RAR well knew.[39] In 1973, Rhodesia had time, but by 1977, when efforts to secure the PVs were stepped up and Guard Force was formed, time was up and the insurgents had the upper hand in the tribal areas.

Selous Scouts

By 1973, the Rhodesian Army realized that it had a real problem gathering actionable military intelligence on insurgent locations and activities. Until Operation Hurricane, counterinsurgency operations relied on intelligence primarily gathered by BSAP and Special Branch from willing locals. Due to the insurgents' shift to a Maoist strategy of coercion and intimidation of local populations, intelligence sources dried up almost completely in 1971, and something had to be done to get RSF back into action. The Rhodesians studied two very effective examples to accomplish this: the British experience against Mau-Mau guerrillas in Kenya, and the Portuguese example of the *fleches*,[40] a unit made up of local tribesmen and turned insurgents used to great effect in Angola and Mozambique. Patterned after these examples, small groups of Rhodesian soldiers, with turned ZIPRA and ZANLA insurgents integrated into their organization, formed into gangs that imitated insurgent tactics to discover the support network and track movements of real insurgent groups. These experiments resulted in tremendous success, and the army formed a regiment to further develop and implement these "pseudo" operations in Rhodesian strategy. The regiment was called the Selous Scouts, named after the renowned Rhodesian hunter, Frederick Courtney Selous.[41]

The Selous Scouts' newly appointed CO, Lieutenant Colonel Ron Reid-Daly, was given top priority on selecting, equipping, and training personnel-black and white-from across the RSF. Recruitment for the Scouts was universal: anyone from any regiment could volunteer for selection, and no unit could refuse such a request. This resulted in some friction between the RAR and Selous Scouts, as Reid-Daly recruited heavily from the RAR to fill his ranks. For the RAR soldiers, selection to the Scouts meant more adventure in a special operations unit, more prestige as a highly trained special operator, and a significant increase in pay. The Selous Scouts offered equal pay for black and white members (unlike any other Rhodesian unit at the time), and they offered the additional incentive of a "special unit allowance"-an extra Rh$1.20 a day, which effectively made the average black Scout's pay the same as the RSM of an RAR rifle battalion. As a result, the Selous Scouts tended to draw out top-performing

NCOs from the RAR, placing the regiment in competition with Reid-Daly's recruiters.[42]

The RAR was not the only source for black Selous Scouts, however. Many were also drawn from the BSAP, SB, and a great many were captured, "tame" insurgents whose experience in ZANLA and ZIPRA was critical to the Scouts' infiltration of the insurgents' networks. Many of the former RAR NCOs served with great distinction as Selous Scouts. While serving with the Scouts, former RAR soldiers earned seven Silver Crosses of Rhodesia, twenty-four Bronze Crosses of Rhodesia, one Member of the Legion of Merit, one Defence Forces Medal for Meritorious Service and thirteen Military Forces Commendations. Two of these men earned both the Silver and Bronze Crosses of Rhodesia, making them the most highly decorated NCOs in the Rhodesian Army.[43] As Reid-Daly stated in *The War Diaries of Andre Dennison*:

> Relations between the RAR and the Selous Scouts were not always cordial during the Rhodesian war. That is perfectly understandable from the RAR point of view, for they had to stand by and watch many of their best men poached for the Selous Scouts. But if one looks back dispassionately now, free from the stress and tensions brought about by the war, officers and soldiers of the RAR must only feel pride in the many deeds of valour performed by their men who served with great courage and distinction in the Selous Scouts.[44]

One Selous Scouts officer interviewed for this study recalled his selection course, which 175 candidates started, from whom only 12 were selected. At the tender age of 38, this officer struggled to finish the final forced march of the course, a tremendously long journey with full kit. He stopped to rest his aching feet, nearly at the end of his endurance, and a fellow candidate from the RAR stopped with him, picked up his rucksack and finished alongside the officer, carrying his own pack and the officer's the rest of the way. Such was the selflessness and spirit of these men. To be sure, the RAR was not the sole reason for the astounding success of the Selous Scouts, but "without the men of the RAR, the Scouts would not have been half as effective."[45]

Fireforce

How do you force the guerrilla into confrontation situations (contacts) on your own terms, given the fact that the enemy's tactics and training make him adept at avoiding these situations?... Army actions alone (ambushes and fleeting contacts) seldom result in the guerrilla suffering significant casualties and follow-up operations on foot using trackers are also of dubious value.... Air power used in isolation is similarly ineffective. In order to locate the guerrilla and force him to fight (or surrender), the peculiar attributes of ground and air forces acting in concert are required. Employed in the appropriate manner they provide the best possible chance of inflicting heavy casualties, and combined they provide a formidable fighting force.[46]

To act on the real-time intelligence gathered by the Selous Scouts and others, the Rhodesian Army needed a rapid reaction force on standby, with coordinated air support and ground troops ready to rapidly attack and destroy identified cells of terrorists before they could escape. To this end, the SAS began experimenting with dropping paratroops in Tête province of Mozambique to vertically envelop targeted insurgent groups. These experiments, combined with the refined insertion of heliborne troops from RhAF Alouette helicopters, led to the deployment of the first "fireforce" at Centenary in January 1974.[47]

Early fireforce deployments consisted of several groups of four men, called sticks. In each stick was "a junior officer, NCO or senior trooper, armed with an FN rifle and equipped with a VHF A63/76 radio; two riflemen, one with first aid training; and a machine gunner carrying a MAG 7.62mm machine gun."[48] An Alouette helicopter could carry one stick of soldiers-the troop-carrying helicopters were called "G-Cars." The fireforce commander, usually the company or troop commander or 2IC, rode in a command helicopter, called a "K-Car." The fireforce commander was responsible for spotting terrorists on the ground, talking to the Observation Post (OP), coordinating all troop deployments, and integrating airstrikes from bombers and Lynx[49] aircraft with ground operations, while the K-Car pilot coordinated all helicopter movements and kept his aircraft in the fight. Within a few months of starting fireforce deployments (by June 1974) K-Cars were also equipped with 20mm Matra cannons, and were able to effectively engage ground targets while circling over the contact at 800 feet.[50]

Several sticks were deployed according to direction from the fireforce commander circling overhead in the K-Car. These sticks would serve as "stop groups" while another group (one or several sticks, depending on the situation) acted as a "sweep group," tasked to clear the open area to flush their quarry into an ambush at the stop group locations. The circling K-Car provided fire support from its mounted gun, and coordinated strikes from Lynx and other aircraft.[51]

On 15 February 1974, the efforts of establishing fireforce were rewarded as 20 RLI soldiers were called in and arrived on five Alouette helicopters to assault an insurgent camp discovered by an Air Force pilot near Mount Darwin. Later that same month, one of the first Selous Scouts operations led by Lieutenant Dale Collett infiltrated a large group of ZANLA cadre operating in Rhodesia. By 18 April 1975, Lt. Collett's group had enough intelligence to call in a fireforce. Once again, the fireforce at Centenary-this time from B Company 1RAR-arrived and surrounded the insurgents. The final result of this contact was 7 insurgents killed, 5 captured (one of whom died later), and 7 escaped (two of whom were believed wounded). Another body was found three weeks later. The results of these early fireforce operations were encouraging to the RAR and the RSF in general.[52]

There were lessons yet to be learned in employment of fireforce, and the weapons and tactics would continue to evolve for the rest of the war-notably with the addition of 20mm Matra cannons to the Alouette gunships (called K-Cars) in June 1974, and the use of DC-3 Dakotas to drop paratroops in 1977 (until 1977 only the SAS were parachute qualified). The concept began with four or five sticks of troopers deploying by helicopter with additional sticks arriving via ground convoy (called the "land tail"), and would eventually evolve into large packages of hundreds of soldiers employed in "jumbo" fireforces conducting external raids into Zambia and Mozambique. The size of the Fireforce was determined by the size of the enemy and the situation on the ground.[53]

The RLI and RAR were the principal units to execute fireforce operations. RLI commandos and RAR companies rotated through fireforce deployments at forward airfields scattered throughout the operational areas of the country. In later "jumbo" fireforce raids into Zambia and Mozambique the RLI and SAS operated almost exclusively, while the RAR tended to execute internal fireforce operations (that is, within the country of Rhodesia). This was because the RAR was generally better at pursuing insurgents through the tribal areas while operating amongst the population to gain intelligence and look for inconsistencies. The RLI's strengths-aggressive, fast-paced, initiative driven contact-were much better suited to external operations.[54]

Between Selous Scouts and fireforce, RSF made the innovations necessary to counter the Phase Two tactical shift to Maoist principles that ZANLA made in 1972. By the end of 1974, there were only 60-70 insurgents left operating in Rhodesia, all contained in the northeast part of the country and vastly outnumbered by the RSF. Militarily, Rhodesia had regained the military advantage and had the insurgents pressed nearly to the breaking point. The population had been moved into PVs in much of the area identified as insurgent stronghold, isolating them (temporarily) from insurgent influence.[55]

Loss of an ally: Portugal withdraws from Africa

On 25 April 1974, the Portuguese Army in Lisbon staged a *coup d'état* (the Carnation Revolution) and took over the government. The new government in Lisbon, made up largely of disillusioned army officers tired of fighting costly colonial wars in Africa, promptly granted independence to all of its African colonies, and on 25 July 1974 Mozambique was turned over to FRELIMO as over 250,000 Portuguese inhabitants fled the country.[56]

The Portuguese withdrawal and the subsequent takeover of Mozambique by FRELIMO was a strategic disaster for Rhodesia. Portugal was a crucial ally to the Rhodesian government. They offered military cooperation, trade and access to ports on the Indian Ocean. Despite their tactical ineptitude and relatively poor military attributes,[57] the Portuguese had been fighting a counterinsurgency much longer than their Rhodesian counterparts, and the Rhodesians learned much about what to do (and what not to do) from their Portuguese allies and neighbors. In fact, the Portuguese contribution to joint military discussions were crucial in developing the early Rhodesian responses to nationalist insurgent operations. PVs and pseudo operations were both patterned after Portuguese examples (the former, unfortunately, was patterned more closely than it should have been). The formation of Grey's Scouts, a mounted infantry unit, as an effective counterinsurgency force was also a Rhodesian idea with Portuguese precedent.[58]

Without Portuguese Mozambique, Rhodesia only had South Africa to turn to for assistance, and that put the Rhodesian government at the mercy of its southern neighbor, under tremendous pressure of its own. As the new government of Mozambique, FRELIMO-already allied with ZANLA by tribal ties and as a fellow nationalist group-subsequently offered its direct assistance, bases and safe haven throughout Mozambique. FRELIMO ceased all assistance to the Rhodesian government, enforced the UN Embargo, and closed its ports to Rhodesian cargo. With FRELIMO assistance (and without Portuguese Army interference) ZANLA had unrestricted access to Mozambique and another 1,100 kilometers of border along which to stage incursions and strikes. The Rhodesian Army and the RAR would soon have an unsolvable problem on their eastern frontier- it would later prove no longer possible to militarily contain the growing insurgency.[59]

Conclusion

Those developments were yet to come, however. By the end of the second phase of the Bush War, RSF had overcome the insurgents' shift to a Maoist strategy by establishing the first permanent JOC in Operation Hurricane, and by adapting new tactics to isolate the population, increase intelligence and act decisively when that intelligence revealed a valid target. At the end of 1974, as at the end of 1971, Rhodesia had the war very much in hand militarily. This would not continue. The loss of the friendly Portuguese government in Mozambique increased regional pressure on Rhodesia, and left the Rhodesian Front government with very few options. From this point forward, factors beyond Rhodesian control would drive the pace of the war.

For its part, the RAR remained steadily and increasingly employed throughout this period. The advent of fireforce increased demands on the regiment. The RAR had learned valuable lessons since Operation Nickel, and proved its effectiveness in conducting fireforce operations, patrols, and observation post missions against an increasingly familiar ZANLA opponent.

The political uncertainties of the Pearce Commission and increased insurgent intimidation in the tribal areas and *kraals* had surprisingly little effect on the availability of black volunteers for service in the regiment. While never explicitly employed in securing Protected Villages, the RAR could have provided a valuable service by committing to the development of PV security forces during this critical period. Later attempts to secure PVs (discussed in subsequent chapters) would be hastily conceived and poorly executed.

With the formation of the Selous Scouts, many of the best NCOs left the RAR for better pay and more adventure as trackers and pseudo operators under Lt. Col. Reid-Daly. While the loss of these NCOs did degrade 1RAR slightly, the regiment still retained its reputation as a superb counterinsurgency force and did not suffer tremendously.

The loss of Portuguese influence in Mozambique would have profound effects on the RAR, as the increased tempo of the war stretched its companies more thinly across a wider area of the country. The numbers of insurgents encountered by fireforce operations would quickly increase from dozens to hundreds, while the RLI and SAS strikes targeted thousands of insurgents in external raids.

Notes

1. These operational areas were permanent JOCs with attached subordinate units from RSF. The size of RSF forces in each operational area varied with the level of activity in them, but generally consisted of several infantry companies and sliced elements of BSAP, Special Branch, Selous Scouts, RhAF and any other security forces required for operations.

2. Wood, *Counterstrike*, 37-39.

3. Wood, 39.

4. Colonial Relations Office to Prime Minister of Southern Rhodesia, 21 September 1965, as found in Hyam, 369-70.

5. Hyam, 370.

6. Smith, 156. Smith (then Prime Minister of Rhodesia) suggests other reasons Britain did not grant Rhodesian independence. Chiefly, he states that the British government under Harold Wilson and the Labour Party was motivated to support black nationalists by its desire to "appease the OAU," while Ted Heath's Conservative Party, which won the 1970 British general election, was more interested in obtaining British entry into the European Economic Community than solving the Rhodesian problem. Whatever the reason, British attitudes regarding Rhodesian recognition certainly differed between Salisbury and London, and between the Colonial Office, Foreign Office and Prime Minister in both Labour and Conservative governments. The resulting duplicity of Her Majesty's Government confused both the Rhodesian government and black nationalist movements.

7. Patrick O'Meara, *Rhodesia: Racial Conflict or Coexistence* (Ithaca: Cornell University Press, 1975), 15.

8. O'Meara, 40-54; Smith, 151-2; Nyangoni, 57-8; Martin, 68-9.

9. Smith, 151; O'Meara, 43. The 1969 "UDI" constitution also amended the Assembly seat allocation to 50 A roll, 8 B roll, and another 8 seats to be nominated by tribal chiefs. The cross-voting concept was removed, and the B roll was explicitly designated for "non-European" voters. For the first time, Rhodesian voter rolls were explicitly racially divided. The UDI constitution provided a means to increase the number of B roll seats in tandem with the increase in blacks meeting the standards for the higher roll (higher education, property and income tax contributions), up to parity at 50 B roll seats. Then, once blacks reached parity with whites, "a committee would be appointed to decide how to bring about an African majority government, and their suggestions would require approval by two-thirds of Parliament (essentially giving the white minority a veto power)." Ian Smith disagreed with the idea of racial division, believing that Rhodesia should "perpetuate the principle and continue our philosophy of trying to establish a genuine meritocracy in keeping with Rhodes's famous dictum: 'Equal rights for all civilised men.'" His efforts to exclude racial divisions were not accepted by the rest of the Rhodesian Front,

and the racial language, which had not been in the Rhodesian constitution since the 1952 Federal constitution, remained in the 1969 document. In March 1970, a general election placed the UDI constitution into effect and formed the Rhodesian government into a republic, with explicitly racial division of voter rolls.

10. Smith, 152.

11. O'Meara, 42.

12. Smith, 153.

13. O'Meara, 46-7.

14. J. K. Cilliers, *Counter-Insurgency in Rhodesia* (Dover: Croom Helm, 1985), 11. The ANC was formed by Bishop Abel Muzurewa (also spelled Muzorewa) in 1971 with the expressed purpose of actively encouraging black Rhodesians to reject the Home-Smith Agreement. In this endeavor, it was highly successful, as described here. The ANC, unlike ZAPU and ZANU, never formed a military arm to take up arms against the Rhodesian government, and so was never banned from participating in Rhodesian politics. Muzurewa would come to be seen as a moderate nationalist leader, and would engage in talks over the next few years with the Smith government, ending in the Internal Settlement of March, 1978 and the establishment of majority rule in Rhodesia-Zimbabwe.

15. Smith, 156; O'Meara, 54; Cilliers, 11; Kriger, 86; Wood, *Counterstrike*, 35; Lester A. Sobel, ed., *Rhodesia/Zimbabwe 1971-77* (New York: Facts on File, 1978), 30-1.

16. Smith. Smith's estimation of the percentage of Africans polled by the Pearce Commission (5 percent) differs from other accounts, which place the number at 6 percent. The discrepancy is noted here because Smith is quoted directly. Most other sources support the 6 percent number. Regardless, the Pearce Commission only met with a tiny sample of African population after much violence surrounding their arrival from both ANC activists and Rhodesian police. The Pearce Commission report acknowledged that fact but believed they had captured the predominant feeling of the black population, much to the consternation of Smith and the Rhodesian Front.

17. Wellington W. Nyangoni. *African Nationalism In Zimbabwe (Rhodesia)* (Washington, DC: University Press of America, 1977), 89.

18. CE20110908G0001, former RAR officer, interview; CE20110908M0001, former RAR officer, interview.

19. David Martin and Phyllis Johnson, *The Struggle for Zimbabwe* (London: Faber and Faber, 1981), 73.

20. Binda, *Masodja*, 248; Wood, *Counterstrike*, 38; Martin, 73.

21. Binda, *Masodja*, 262-3; Wood, *Counterstrike*, 38; Martin, 146.

22. FRELIMO (*Frente de Libertaçao de Moçambique*), or Liberation Front

of Mozambique, was the communist insurgent group in Mozambique fighting against the ruling Portuguese government. Because of their tribal similarities (the western portion of Mozambique was predominantly inhabited by Shona tribes) ZANU and ZANLA were able to make great allies of FRELIMO, using their bases for training, staging and operating extensively. ZAPU tended to operate out of Zambia throughout the war.

23. Martin, 97.

24. These were open areas for RSF to engage the insurgents without placing the population at risk by moving selected rural populations into consolidated compounds

25. Cilliers, 101.

26. Binda, *Masodja*, 265; CE20110909R0001, former RAR officer, interview; CE20110913M0001, former RAR officer, interview. By this point, Rhodesian Army planners were working in Pretoria with both Portuguese and South African counterparts to drive policy decisions and compare experiences. Called Exercise Alcora, these planning sessions were largely influenced by the Portuguese contingent until their sudden withdrawal in 1974 (following the coup in Lisbon). Portugal was seen as the most experienced counterinsurgent force of the three parties involved. Once the Portuguese withdrew, the sessions became known as Exercise Oryx, and Rhodesian and South African military planners continued to meet in Pretoria.

27. John P. Cann, *Counterinsurgency in Africa: The Portuguese Way of War 1961-1974* (Westport, CT: Greenwood Press, 1997), 159.

28. Robert Thompson, *Defeating Communist Insurgency* (St. Petersburg, FL: Hailer, 2005), 124-5. Thompson refers to "strategic hamlets" to describe this concept. A veteran of Malaya himself, Thompson was also influential in adapting this theory for US commanders in Vietnam, where US and Vietnamese forces also attempted a strategic hamlet program, with minimal success. The concept is to create pockets of security and safety inside contested areas, allowing popular support to grow due to favorable security conditions, while denying resources and assistance to the insurgents. American counterinsurgency theorist John McCuen also describes this as the "oil spot strategy" in his book, *The Art of Counter-Revolutionary War*.

29. Cilliers, 99.

30. Cilliers., 82. De Kock used the term "no-go areas" in his statement, which are defined in Rhodesian Army manual, *Military Support to the Civil Power,* as areas "from which all civilians are excluded by an order of the Protecting Authority, in terms of Section 4(1)(b) of the Emergency Powers (Maintenance of Law and Order) regulations
. . . in order to ensure that they do not become involved in operations conducted by Security Forces against terrorists. Only authorised members of the Security Forces, on duty, will move in no-go areas and no action may be instituted against

them for any death or any act performed in good faith in the course of operations conducted during the time whilst the order is in force."

31.   Cilliers, 84.

32.   Cilliers, 82-4.

33.   Cilliers, 99.

34.   Cilliers. Internal Affairs was the ministry of the Rhodesian government charged with administering the tribal areas. They were the lead agency for instituting the PV program, with the military in support.

35.   Cilliers, 85.

36.   Cilliers, 99.

37.   Cilliers, 88.

38.   CE20110912G0001, former RAR officer, interview; CG20110927S0001, former RAR officer, interview. In one interview, a former RAR officer said that he was placed in charge of *pfomu re vanhu* in 1979. On his assignment to work with *pfomu re vanhu*, this officer said that he had very little direction, and no understanding of what the intention was with the men he was to train. He-then a Lieutenant-and his CSM were given the task of developing a six-week program to conduct basic military training, then pushing the trainees out as quickly as possible.

39.   CE20110912G0001, former RAR officer, interview. See later discussion on SFAs. After initial training by Selous Scouts, the SFA program was run by officers of 1RAR. Guard Force was formed by Brigadier Bill Godwin, former CO 1RAR, brought out of retirement by Rhodesian Army HQ for the task.

40.   Former Selous Scouts officer, interview by author, 10 November 2011; Reid-Daly, *Top Secret War*, 109-11, 120. In standing up the Selous Scouts, Lt Col Reid-Daly admits openly to both the British and Portuguese influences. In fact, both British and Portuguese officers were directly involved with the development of Selous Scouts concept. Lieutenant Spike Powell, who worked in pseudo operations in Kenya (and was later killed in the second Air Rhodesia Viscount shot down by ZIPRA in 1979) collaborated in the early pseudo operations experiments in Rhodesia (as early as 1966), and Reid-Daly personally visited the *flechas* compound at Vila Pery (Chimoio), Mozambique, to study their methods and tactics. Colonel Oscar Cordosa, commander of the *flechas*, would later lead several of his men into Rhodesia to join the Selous Scouts after FRELIMO took over Mozambique in 1974.

41.   Reid-Daly, *Top Secret War*, 65-69. Selous, an Englishman, arrived in Africa in 1871 at the age of 19. He hunted elephants and other big game in what would later become Rhodesia, and was widely respected by the Ndebele and several notable characters, such as avid big game hunter and US President Theodore Roosevelt, Kaiser Wilhelm I and author Rider Haggard. Haggard later

immortalized Selous as Alan Quartermain, the hero of *King Solomon's Mines*. At the outbreak of World War I in 1914, he attempted to join the army but was rejected because of his age (he was 62). However, he was later recruited by the War Office after it was determined that the Brits were losing too many men to the bush and diseases while chasing down German forces in East Africa. Finally brought into service and commissioned as a Lieutenant, Selous was a tremendous asset to the British army, but was killed by a stray bullet in a skirmish near the Rufiji River in Uganda. Out of respect for his mastery and love of the African bush, he was buried where he fell and his grave stands today on a game reserve which bears his name.

42. Reid-Daly., 102-7. In his book, Reid-Daly describes an "insidious plot" within the RAR to undermine his recruiting efforts. After his initial recruiting drive, he received word that 90 percent of the candidates from the RAR had withdrawn their applications. At Reid-Daly's insistence, Army HQ subsequently ordered all who applied to go to selection, and Reid-Daly offered the candidates the opportunity to choose between the Selous Scouts and the RAR at the end of selection. Few chose to leave the Scouts.

43. Reid-Daly, *Challenge*, 155.

44. Wood, *War Diaries*, xii.

45. CB20111110S0001, former Selous Scouts officer, interview by author, Fort Leavenworth, Kansas, 10 November 2011.

46. Wing Commander Peter R. Briscoe, as quoted in Alexandre Binda's *The Saints*.

47. Wood, *Counterstrike*, 90.

48. Wood, 102.

49. A Lynx was a Cessna 337, armed with .30 caliber cannons and rockets. Lynxes were crucial enablers for Fireforce action, able to move in, stay low over a target area for a long period of time and provide immediate, accurate airstrikes when required, as well as guide in attacks from other strike aircraft.

50. Wood, *Counterstrike*, 96-103.

51. The RhAF was able to employ an aging and tiny fleet of ground attack aircraft with tremendous effect on the battlefield. These included Hawker-Hunter FGA9 ground attack fighters, Vampire FB52 fighters, English Electric Canberra B2 light bombers, Provost trainers (adapted to carry .303 machine guns and napalm bombs). Sales of aircraft, engines and repair parts were the first round of sanctions imposed on Rhodesia by the United Nations after UDI, and so the fact that these aircraft continued flying throughout the war is a testament to the ingenuity and resourcefulness of the Rhodesian Air Force "blue jobs."

52. Binda, *Masodja*, 265-6; Wood, *Counterstrike*, 91. Wood describes this action as a disappointment due to the RAR commander landing during the fight to direct action from the ground. Regardless, the results of this Fireforce, like

the previous action of the RLI, resulted in higher insurgent kill rates than had been achieved prior to Fireforce. The RAR, like the rest of the Rhodesian Army, would continue to improve and adapt from this action.

53. Wood, *Counterstrike*, 91-2. The DC-3 Dakota, called the "Paradak," could deliver up to 20 paratroops at a time. The Rhodesian use of paratroops in Fireforce was born of necessity, due to a shortage of helicopters: one Paradak delivered the same number of troops as five Alouette helicopters, and increasing numbers of Fireforce callouts against larger groups of insurgents called for airborne insertion in addition to heliborne insertion just to get enough forces on the ground to handle the situation.

54. CE20110909T0001, former RAR officer, interview; Wood, *Counterstrike*, 96.

55. Cilliers, 21-2; Wood, *Counterstrike*, 39; Trevor Desfountain, summary and background notes of a 1979 Rhodesian Strategy Revision Conference, compiled in 1984. Cilliers and Wood disagree on the number of insurgents operating in Rhodesia at the end of 1974. Wood cites that there were 60, Cilliers that there were 70. At any rate, the number was small, and the insurgents had lost the military edge they had started to gain with the attacks in Chiweshi in 1972.

56. Binda, *Masodja*, 266.

57. Al J. Ventner, "Why Portugal Lost Its African Wars," in *Challenge: Southern Africa within the African Revolutionary context* (Gibraltar: Ashanti, 1989), . Rhodesians who worked with their Portuguese counterparts in Mozambique saw little military competence or bushcraft in the largely metropolitan Portuguese Army. With notable exceptions, such as the *flechas*, most Portuguese soldiers had little knowledge and less interest in African affairs, and their attitude was manifest in their lack of military intensity. Nonetheless, Portuguese withdrawal from Mozambique, and the subsequent turnover of governance to FRELIMO, was a tremendous loss for Rhodesia.

58. CE20110909R0001, former RAR officer, interview; CE20110913M0001, former Grey's Scouts officer, interview; Cann, 139. Exercise Alcora was a crucial joint collaborative effort between Rhodesian, South African, and Portuguese military planners, in which the Portuguese had the leading role. Portuguese dragoons, or *dragões*, began operating in Silva Porto, Angola in 1966 and by 1971 were also in Mozambique. This idea predated Grey's Scouts, a Rhodesian mounted infantry unit formed in 1976. The use of horse-mounted troops in the southern African bush was highly effective.

59. Cilliers, 19-20; Binda, *Masodja*, 266.

Chapter 5
Phase Three: 1974-1977

Phase three of the war, from 1974-77, initially saw a negotiated détente and a ceasefire brokered by South African Prime Minister John Vorster during a December 1974 conference with the "frontline" states of Zambia, Tanzania, Botswana, Angola and Mozambique. This ceasefire was quickly broken by ZANU and ZAPU, and the war intensified again through 1976. ZANLA and ZIPRA continued to build strength and recruit from among the black rural population, as large numbers of whites, mostly from the urban centers, began to leave the country. Rhodesian forces responded to the insurgent violation of the ceasefire agreements by attacking into Zambia and Mozambique, targeting ZIPRA and ZANLA base camps. To control a growing military operation within and outside of Rhodesian borders, Ian Smith established a Combined Operations (ComOps) organization, deploying increasing numbers of security forces and striving to "contain the war.[1]

The increased demands on security forces caused the Rhodesian government to create a second battalion of RAR, among other changes to National Service and Territorial Force structures. This period also saw the commissioning of the first black officers in June 1977, followed by parachute training for both RAR and RLI soldiers later that same year. Political activity was marked by increased outside political pressure from South Africa, Britain and the United States to force Rhodesia towards majority rule.[2]

Détente

In late 1974 South African Prime Minister John Vorster agreed to enter into a détente with the front-line states to resolve the situation in Rhodesia. The aim was to unite ZANU, ZAPU and ANC under the leadership of Bishop Abel Muzorewa, and then to negotiate a settlement between the united nationalist movements and Smith's government. If this scheme worked, the front-line states promised to recognize white-rule South Africa, buying the apartheid government time and influence among its neighbors, albeit at the Rhodesia's expense. The terms of the ceasefire-as dictated by the leaders of Zambia, Mozambique and Tanzania-were an immediate end to hostilities, withdrawal of South African forces from Rhodesia, the lifting of bans on ZANU and ZAPU, and release of political detainees. The released nationalist leaders and Smith's government would attend a constitutional conference in Lusaka to negotiate the transfer of power in Rhodesia to majority rule. In exchange for these terms, the frontline states would use their influence to discourage ZANLA and ZIPRA military actions in Rhodesia; prevent incursions from frontline states into South Africa; bring Nkomo, Sithole and Mugabe to the negotiating table; and host the Lusaka conference.[3]

Ian Smith's Rhodesian Front government, still attempting to cope with the loss of its eastern trading partner and ally, and facing a five-fold increase in its front line (which now included the entire Mozambique border, as well as the Zambia and Botswana borders), had little choice but to accept the terms of détente. Refusal of these terms would have cut crucial ties with South Africa and completely isolated Rhodesia. So, on 11 December 1974, Smith agreed to the ceasefire and released all detainees, among whom were Joshua Nkomo (ZAPU), Ndabaningi Sithole (ZANU), and Robert Mugabe (ZANU). RSF pulled back and stopped pursuing insurgents in Rhodesia. The consequences of this would prove disastrous. In discussing the détente, Smith said:

> We were on the brink of dealing them a knock-out blow-we had them on the run-of this we had no doubt. In our minds, the détente exercise undoubtedly saved those terrorists remaining in Rhodesia because our security forces abided by the terms of the ceasefire. We pulled back in order to give the terrorists time to comply with their part of the bargain. However, before long it became clear the enemy had no intention of keeping its promise. This not only affected us militarily, but, more importantly, psychologically. The terrorists cashed in on our withdrawal by telling the locals that they had won the war and that we were retreating. Our actions (and those of the departing South African police units) substantiated their claims. This was probably the most important aspect of all.[4]

Smith was right-ZANLA was nearly militarily defeated before the détente. Fighting in the northeast during Operation Hurricane had taken its toll on trained insurgent fighters and leaders, and the nationalist movement was starting to melt down-not without some assistance from Rhodesian Central Intelligence Organization (CIO). In November 1974, a rebellion broke out within the ranks of ZANLA over the detached lifestyle of the ZANU and ZANLA leadership in Lusaka, lack of supplies and poor administration of the war. While newly recruited ZANLA soldiers fought and died in Rhodesia, some of the ground commanders for ZANLA saw their leaders' opulent lifestyles outside the country as hypocrisy. Called the Nhari Rebellion, this revolt was ultimately put down by the ZANU Chief of Defense, Joseph Tongogara.[5] The two leaders of the Nhari Rebellion were executed, along with others. A few months later, in March 1975, ZANU

Chairman Herbert Chitepo was also assassinated in Lusaka.[6] Between the Nhari Rebellion, Chitepo's assassination, and subsequent rivalry amongst ZANU members, the Zambian government soon tired of ZANU. By 28 March, Zambia arrested most of ZANU's members in the country and closed their offices, saying ZANU were "prejudicial to the maintenance of peace, order and good government."[7]

After this humiliation of ZANU's leadership and Zambia's refusal to continue to support their movement, the remaining ZANU members in Zambia fled to Mozambique. This left the Rhodesian nationalist movement in Zambia exclusively to ZAPU and ZIPRA. Additionally, the OAU now insisted on funneling its funding through Muzorewa's ANC, so resources, logistics, and leadership for ZANLA were all getting even more scarce in 1975. The new chairman for ZANU, Robert Mugabe, began to establish himself and his organization in Mozambique. This move temporarily shut down ZANU operations in Rhodesia for much of the year. By Rhodesian intelligence estimates, in December 1975 there were only three groups of 10 ZANLA insurgents each operating in Rhodesia.[8]

Then an idea surfaced among the nationalists to form a "third force," to unite ZIPRA and ZANLA into one organization committed to the armed struggle for the liberation of blacks in Rhodesia. Led by Rex Nhongo (ZANLA) and Alfred "Nikita" Mangena (ZIPRA), this organization called itself the Zimbabwe People's Army (ZIPA). While the union lasted quite briefly, ZIPA did carry out attacks along the new open border between Manicaland (in eastern Rhodesia) and Mozambique. In response to these attacks, Rhodesia established Operation Thrasher in February 1976, based out of Umtali, and increased call-ups among Rhodesian army reserves. This increased activity also led to the creation of a second RAR battalion. 2RAR, like 1RAR, was completely filled by black volunteers. Many more potential recruits were still turning out to enlist in the RAR than could be accepted.[9]

2RAR

At the breakup of the Central African Federation in 1963, the Rhodesian Army recommended to the government that the RAR be comprised of two battalions with three line companies each. The idea was that it would be much easier to grow each battalion to accommodate four or five rifle companies and a support company, should the need arise, than to build a new battalion on short notice-potentially in the middle of a war. The Rhodesian government refused this request, and decided instead to keep the RAR strength at one battalion, adding a fifth company, "E" Company, in 1964. "Regrettably, the Rhodesian Front did not trust the African soldier."[10]

Distrust of black soldiers had two principal sources: past experience during the establishment of Rhodesia, and the Congo Crisis of 1961. After the tribal uprisings of the 1890s, Rhodesia was wary of creating a black regiment (the RNR), for fear that a trained, armed force of blacks could easily overthrow the relatively small white security forces-many of whom had personally experienced the events of the 1890s. The RNR exhibited no such tendencies however; nor did the RAR during any part of its existence. Suspicions of black troops rose again in June 1960 with news of the Congo Crisis. In the southern Congo region of Katanga, black soldiers of the *Force Publique* mutinied against their white officers and "attacked local white civilians, looting, raping, and inciting a mass exodus of Belgian officers, administrators and settlers during the summer of 1960." The fear of a black mutiny on the heels of the Congo Crisis led to the creation of all-white regular army units in the Central African Federation-the RLI, SAS, and Armored Car Regiment-to balance the four "African" battalions in the Federal Army (the NRR, two battalions of KAR, and the RAR). This move was to mitigate a perceived vulnerability of the white population against a similar mutiny in the Central African Federation amidst "subversive activities of nationalists in Nyasaland and Northern Rhodesia." This fear was not founded in any evidence of such activity in the RAR, but seemed to be the source of hesitation in the Rhodesian government to follow the army's recommendation and create additional RAR battalions early on.[11]

Once the Bush War began, in the late 1960s, the Rhodesian government also failed to:

> heed warnings from the army that, despite the presence of two 100-man companies of South African police, its regular component was overstretched when merely assisting the BSAP with border control. The retired former Federal Prime Minister, Sir Roy Welensky, suggested raising 10 RAR battalions, but, because the immediate threat seemed so minor, and funds were short, the Treasury and the Department of Defense were fatally deaf to all pleas.[12]

It took the government over a decade to realize that more black troops were absolutely necessary to keep up with the demands of the war. By 1975, Rhodesia could no longer sustain the notion that black troops were an unnecessary risk.

In the early part of 1975, accurately predicting imminent increasing demands for troops after FRELIMO took power in Mozambique, the RAR began to form the nucleus of a new battalion by increasing the number of trainees at their training wing. These 230 recruits passed out in July and formed "A" Company, 2nd Battalion RAR (2RAR), under the command of Major André Dennison.[13]

The battalion, commanded by Lieutenant Colonel Peter Hosking, adopted the motto "*Tinowira Kukunda*," which meant "We fight to win." 2RAR was tasked to rapidly form and immediately commence operations, based out of Fort Victoria in the central-eastern part of the country. E Company 1RAR was entirely transferred over to form C Company 2RAR, and B Company 2RAR formed shortly after with recruits passing out of the newly established Depot RAR. By November 1975, A Company 2RAR was deployed around Chipinga, in the Manicaland province along the southeastern border of Rhodesia. These were the initial stages of what would become Operation Thrasher. The formation of 2RAR was a tremendous undertaking, as 1RAR provided most of the NCO leadership for the new battalion. That this endeavor was completed with minimal impact on continuing operations, and that 2RAR was immediately available as a combat force is a testament to the professionalism, training, and leadership of the RAR. It also proves that there was still an ample recruiting base for RAR soldiers in 1975, as the additional strength requirements were adequately met with volunteers.[14]

With the shared heritage and leadership between 1RAR and 2RAR, the two battalions naturally had much in common. However, one key difference between the two battalions of RAR, however, as noted by a former 2RAR subaltern, was 2RAR's lack of emphasis on many of the older, more formal colonial British traditions practiced in years past. According to this officer, "we [2RAR] were less regimental" than 1RAR. In 18 months of service with the battalion, for example, this officer only wore his "Number one" dress uniform once, to a funeral for another officer. By this point in the war, 1RAR was not practicing much formality either- both battalions were busy enough fighting the war. But from its inception, 2RAR never had the opportunity to practice many of the formal traditions of its predecessors. Importantly, the business of fighting the war-and the carried-over knowledge of imported NCOs from 1RAR-served as ample replacement for British regimental traditions, and 2RAR never had any problems among race or tribe within its ranks, either. By this point, the soldiers were more concerned with whether or not the man next to them could shoot and perform his duties than whether he was Shona or Ndebele- or whether his boots were properly shined, for that matter.[15]

Figure 1. RAR machine gunner, ready for action.
Source: Alexandre Binda, Masodja: The History of the Rhodesian African Rifles and its forerunner, the Rhodesia Native Regiment (Johannesburg: 30 Degrees South, 2007), 363.

Increased Insurgent Activity and Rhodesian Response

As a result of the increased activity along the Mozambique border, Rhodesian forces established two new Operational Areas in 1976: Thrasher in February, and Repulse in May. In addition to the newly formed 2RAR, additional national service call-ups increased overall troop strength by about 20,000, but the pressure from insurgent activities continued to build through 1976.[16]

With ZIPA attacking further south along the Mozambique border and ZANLA rebuilding itself in border camps in Mozambique, the eyes of the OAU now turned to ZAPU to carry on the nationalist movement. ZAPU had been focused on equipping and training its Soviet-trained ZIPRA forces in Zambia, sending leaders to Soviet Eastern Europe and Cuba for indoctrination and training. They had not conducted any major operations in Rhodesia for quite some time. By mid-1976, the OAU told ZIPRA to start fighting or lose their funding. ZIPRA duly began infiltrating across the Zambezi River in northwest Rhodesia and northeast Botswana. In August 1976, Rhodesian forces established Operation Tangent to counter the increased ZIPRA activity. Thus, in less than one year, RSF operations went from one operational area to four, as insurgents took advantage of the détente and changing circumstances to increase their activity.[17]

Increased operations brought more need for a unified command to manage what was now a nationwide military operation. Rhodesians knew the Malayan example of a "Director of Operations" quite well, and in March 1977, Ian Smith formed the Ministry of Combined Operations somewhat after the Malayan model, appointing Lieutenant General Peter Walls as the Commander of Combined Operations (ComOps). While this resulted in increased coordination, Lt. Gen. Walls was never afforded the same supreme authority over all efforts and agencies as the Director of Operations was in Malaya-he was even outranked within his own organization by the Chief of the Army, Lieutenant General John Hickman. Quite often the ComOps organization bogged down in bureaucratic inertia, as other agencies sent deputies and generally were not bound to obey the directives coming from Lt. Gen. Walls. However, the organization of ComOps, while far from perfect, was a positive step towards unifying the war effort across government agencies at the strategic level.[18]

One of the tendencies of ComOps and the JOC system used by the Rhodesian Army was that battalions seldom operated as entities of their own. Each JOC commanded elements of several different regiments (RAR, RLI, RR, BSAP, Selous Scouts, etc.) attached on rotational duty. In fact, within weeks of assuming command of 2RAR, one former commander was placed in command of the JOC in Chiredzi, where none of his companies were assigned. He didn't see his own troops for several months, during which time they were farmed out to other operational areas.[19]

During one deployment in 1975, D Company 1RAR deployed to an operational area and integrated with a company of national servicemen of the Rhodesia Regiment (RR). For the entire six-week rotation, the two units broke down into integrated teams, and one RR NCO recalled that two of his soldiers, both of Afrikaans descent, drew an assignment to work in a four-man stick under a black RAR corporal with a black RAR lance corporal as a MAG gunner. These two white soldiers each owned farms which employed hundreds of blacks. They were not accustomed at all to taking orders from black men, and initially expressed their hesitation at spending time in the bush under the command of a black NCO. But at the insistence of their own NCO they duly set off for a six week duty with their RAR colleagues.[20]

At the end of six weeks, the RR NCO anxiously waited at the rendezvous for his soldiers to return from their patrol. His curiosity peaked when he saw the RAR corporal walk in from the bush with an extra ruck sack on his back and an extra pair of boots slung over his neck. The RAR lance corporal walked in behind him, also with extra boots and an extra ruck sack in addition to his machine gun. When the RR NCO asked the RAR corporal if he had any problems with the two men, the corporal said, "No, absolutely not." Then, the two white soldiers came staggering in, obviously exhausted, with a new-found respect for their black counterparts. They had learned the ability of the RAR soldiers to conduct extended patrols over long distances in the Rhodesian bush, and had trouble keeping up. They came away with an intimate knowledge of this and learned to respect their black colleagues' capabilities.[21]

External Operations

With ZANLA and ZIPRA establishing camps and assembly areas just across the borders in Zambia and Mozambique, Rhodesia was faced with a military problem common to many counterinsurgency operations. In order to effectively attack the insurgents before they came into the country and dispersed into smaller groups, Rhodesian forces needed to conduct offensive operations within other sovereign nations, namely Zambia and Mozambique. Given the extreme political pressure on the Rhodesian Front government, this was a tough problem to solve. As they had done in the past, the neighboring governments would condemn any such attacks on "refugee camps," and demand further international retribution, which Rhodesia could ill afford (particularly from its only remaining friendly neighbor, South Africa).[22]

In the face of evidence, however, Rhodesia could hardly sit and wait for large groups of insurgents gathering across the borders to enter the country and overwhelm security forces there. In one case, Selous Scouts conducted a reconnaissance between 27 May and 4 June 1976, identifying a large ZANLA-FPLM camp on the Mudzi River, about 30 kilometers inside Mozambique. True to Mao's teaching that "you cannot win at the conference table what you have not won on the battlefield," Mugabe was preparing a massive attack by ZANLA into Rhodesia to coincide with the Geneva Conference, planned for October 1976. According to reports, approximately 2,000 insurgents were operating inside Rhodesia by the end of October, with another 8,000 ready to enter from Mozambique. As one officer described the situation, if Rhodesia allowed the buildup to continue unabated in Mozambique, they would find their current problems to be "the thin end of a very thick and ugly wedge to come."[23]

In response to the intelligence gathered, and to weaken Mugabe's position going into the Geneva Conference, RSF planned Operation Mardon, a set of preemptive attacks to destroy the Mudzi Camp and others, disrupting the logistical support and infiltration routes into northeastern Rhodesia. Shutting down these bases and routes would also force ZANLA to infiltrate further south along the Mozambique border, where terrain favored Rhodesian detection and fireforce operations. In August 1976, the Selous Scouts had conducted a major attack near this area, killing over 1,000 insurgents in a major ZANLA base at Nyadzonya.[24]

Operation Mardon called for SAS, RLI, Grey's Scouts (horse-mounted infantry) and two companies of RAR (D Coy 1RAR and A Coy 2RAR) to simultaneously attack targeted camps on 31 October to maximize surprise and prevent the insurgents' escape. Of all forces involved, D Coy 1RAR had the most success against its target, the Mudzi Camp. After conducting a night march in through extremely difficult terrain under heavy combat loads, D Company arrived at their target, which they believed to be a few dozen ZANLA fighters transiting between other camps. What they found was actually training camp teeming with over 800 ZANLA recruits under the protection of FRELIMO and Tanzanian troops. Unexpected delays in the approach march caused the attack to shift a day later than planned. Without air support (the limited sorties available were supporting strikes on other targets), Lieutenant David Padbury and the 2IC, Captain Glenn Reed (an ex-American Special Forces soldier) planned a hasty attack on the 800 insurgents inside the camp, setting stop groups in ambush on the backside (east side) and a sweep group assaulting across the camp from west to east.[25]

With D Company moving into stop positions on the eastern side of the camp, Padbury set up a command post on the high ground to the west. Capt. Reed began moving the sweep group and mortars into position along a ridge south of Padbury's position, but before the sweep group was in place, a group of Tanzanian soldiers walked into Padbury's position, triggering a premature firefight. The sweep group and mortars quickly moved into position and began to assault across the camp, under effective mortar fire. The stop groups, nearly in their ambush positions, opened fire on the fleeing insurgents. In the ensuing battle, one RAR soldier was burned by a phosphorus grenade and Capt. Reed called for a casevac using fireforce helicopters stationed nearby. The helicopters also provided additional fire support from their guns, as well as observation platforms to spot hidden insurgents. In the end, over 30 insurgents were killed at Mudzi camp, smaller numbers were killed elsewhere during the operation, and Rhodesian forces withdrew, having effectively disrupted the logistical base and infiltration routes in the area.[26]

The RAR only participated in few external operations-notably, Op Mardon and Op Murex later in the war. The great strength of black soldiers in the RAR was in their superior bushcraft and ability to observe and interact with the local population. ComOps tended to employ the RAR inside Rhodesia rather than on the larger raids into Zambia and Mozambique that became defining roles of the RLI and SAS. RAR soldiers, while quite capable of these types of strikes, tended to be less aggressive and more thorough in executing their missions. Their ability to observe and communicate with the population inside Rhodesia was crucial to internal operations.[27]

Parachute Training

By late 1976, increased fireforce actions were starting to reveal the limitations of the small fleet of Rhodesian helicopters. Army Headquarters decided that the only other way to rapidly get troops into a fireforce action was by airborne insertion, and so in late 1977 the RLI and RAR began parachute training. The addition of paratroops to fireforce allowed commanders to get many more troops on the ground in the first wave, resulting in more successful fireforce contacts. The first unit of the RAR to become airborne qualified was B Company 1RAR in October 1977, with the rest of the regiment following closely behind. Initially, there were concerns that black Rhodesian soldiers would not jump out of airplanes, or that their superstitious nature would cause them to panic on the aircraft, but the RAR proved all critics wrong, and were enthusiastic about being airborne. "A" Company 2RAR, under Maj. Dennison's leadership, became one of the most capable and respected fireforce elements in the Rhodesian Army.[28]

RAR soldiers proved themselves capable of every task they were ever asked to do. They participated in fireforce, limited external operations, extended patrols in the bush, and airborne operations. They earned respect for their loyalty, spirit and discipline. But they truly found their strength patrolling the bush, working with the local population, and manning Observation Posts (OPs) for extended periods. They were much more patient and attuned to local customs than their RLI counterparts. In one example, an RAR soldier on an OP with an officer observed three women walking down a path towards a village, one of whom was carrying a suitcase. The white officer thought nothing of it, but the black soldier said, "*Ishe*, the one with the suitcase is a terrorist." "How could you possibly know?" asked the officer. "She is carrying the suitcase in her hand. Our women carry things on their heads." A patrol caught up to the "women," who were in fact insurgents dressed as women walking into a village. This was the strength of the RAR as a counterinsurgent force. They knew the tribes and customs, and could instantly spot what was out of place.[29] On another occasion:

> A group of male civilians, walking along, was spotted from a distance. The [RAR] OP pointed out one of them as an insurgent, even though at first glance nothing distinguished him from the rest of the men. He was picked up, however, and found to be carrying an AK concealed beneath his coat. When quizzed, the RAR soldiers said that they knew he was an insurgent as he swung only one arm when walking (the other held the weapon against his body).[30]

The ability of RAR soldiers to notice and blend into the culture around them, obviously, came from the fact that they grew up in the same culture they were observing. This fact, however, was not always to their advantage, especially when their identity as RAR soldiers was revealed to insurgents operating near their family homes.

Figure 2. RAR paras waiting for a fireforce call-up.
Source: CE20110908G0001, former RAR officer (photo provided by RAR officer).

War on the home front

One of the unfortunate circumstances RAR soldiers (and black soldiers in other units of the Rhodesian army) faced was that their extended families were in the same *kraals*, indeed were the same families, from which the insurgents recruited and relied for support. It was not uncommon, therefore, for an RAR soldier to return to his *kraal* on leave to find insurgents infiltrating his village and intimidating his family. A few soldiers were killed when their identity was known to insurgents. In at least one such incident, however, an RAR private home on leave was able to coordinate, and then participate in, a fireforce on a group of ten insurgents who had arrived in his *kraal* requesting food. Private Wilfred, of A Company 1RAR, reported the "terrs" to a local farmer, providing descriptions of the men in his village that assisted the K-Car in identifying them. Then, he "was given a rifle, webbing and combat jacket and became a member of Stop 1." The subsequent contact killed nine of the ten, and a follow up ambush was set for the tenth insurgent but he was not seen again.[31]

Political Pressure

As the pace of the insurgency increased during 1976, so too did the political pressure on both the Rhodesian government and nationalist sides to compromise and end the conflict. The frontline states were economically affected by the ongoing war, and the OAU was increasingly frustrated by the inconclusive efforts of the nationalist organizations. For their part, Britain wanted to end to an embarrassing problem while maintaining the relevance of the British Commonwealth in Africa. South Africa was looking for a way to gain more time and recognition for its own international pariah of apartheid government. At this point, US Secretary of State Henry Kissinger, the master of "shuttle diplomacy," stepped in to attempt to mediate and bring both sides to an agreement.[32]

Entering Africa on the heels of two embarrassing recent US failures in Vietnam and Angola,[33] Kissinger was eager to:

> co-opt the program of moderate evolutionary reform, that is to say majority rule, and minority rights. At the same time we sought to create a kind of firebreak between those whose radicalism was ideological and those whose radicalism was geared to specific issues. We could meet the demands for majority rule; we never thought we could co-opt the ideological radicals; our goal was to isolate them.[34]

Kissinger had a deadline of his own. By September 1976, it was becoming increasingly apparent that Jimmy Carter would win the upcoming USpresidential elections. This would hurt the process, as any deal brokered by a "lame duck" American administration would expire under the new administration. This American political situation allowed the Patriotic Front to bide their time and see if a better result would come of waiting for the new USpresident.[35]

In September 1976, Kissinger and Vorster invited Ian Smith to Pretoria. In a frank discussion, the two impressed upon Smith that his efforts were doomed to failure if he stayed his course and continued to fight transition to majority rule. They presented a plan, drafted by the British and agreed upon by the frontline states and black Rhodesian nationalists. This plan proposed an interim government, half-white and half-black, to preside over a two year transition to majority rule. Smith's options, as presented by Kissinger and Vorster, were to accept these terms and attend a conference with the nationalist leaders to decide how to implement the plan, or reject the offer and immediately lose all financial and military support from South Africa. Faced with such options, Smith returned to Salisbury and conferred with his cabinet and the caucus, and the Rhodesian government ultimately accepted the terms proposed by Vorster and Kissinger. A conference was set for October 1976 in Geneva to settle the details and set a course for transition to majority rule. Joshua Nkomo, Robert Mugabe and Ndabaningi Sithole all attended the conference. After two months of abortive attempts to reach an agreement, the conference ended with no results. The fighting continued.[36]

Perhaps the greater impact of the Kissinger talks and the Geneva Conference was the revelation of a rift between the South African and Rhodesian governments. This was a new development, and its impact on white Rhodesia, when combined with the prospects of more war, increased national service, and tougher economic times ahead, was devastating. At the end of 1976, the number of whites leaving Rhodesia was greater the number of whites entering the country.[37] The 'white flight' had begun, due in large part to the perception that Rhodesia was friendless and hopeless. This dramatic change in attitude among white Rhodesians would also affect the war in the coming years. Ian Smith observed that the doubts among the white Rhodesian community "were not about the British, Americans, Europeans or the communist-inspired Commonwealth, whom we had known all along we could not trust. Instead, they were about the South Africans, whom we had believed would stand together with us."[38]

Conclusion

This period of the war saw tremendous changes in the Rhodesian Army and the RAR. From its relatively confident position in 1974, the Rhodesian Army was stressed to its limit when the pace of the war increased through 1976. The 1975 détente was a complete failure, which ultimately ceded momentum and initiative over to the insurgents, severely damaging morale across the Rhodesian Army.

Faced with larger groups of insurgents training in safe havens in Zambia and Mozambique, Rhodesia chose a strategy of external strikes against large targets, integrating parachute training across its principal infantry units: the RAR and RLI. Intent on limiting insurgent capacity to infiltrate Rhodesian tribal areas, these external raids increasingly committed a large percentage of the army away from the country, leaving the population even more vulnerable in the tribal areas.

Despite the creation of 2RAR and increased national service commitments, RSF did not have nearly enough troops to secure the population where it was most vulnerable, in the *kraals* and tribal areas and along the borders with Zambia and Mozambique.

Notes

1. Cilliers, 67-8, 197; Wood, *Counterstrike*, 43-4.

2. Binda, *Masodja*, 267-8; Wood, *Counterstrike*, 40-44.

3. Martin, 145.

4. Pat Scully, *Exit Rhodesia* (Ladysmith: Cotswold Press, 1984), 52.

5. Cilliers, 34; CE20110909R0001, former RAR officer, interview. Of note, Many of the "Nhari rebels," including Thomas Nhari, were relatively new commanders recruited from the area of Operation Hurricane, in the northeastern part of Rhodesia. They were Shona, from the KoreKore and Zezuru tribes. Joseph Tongogara and the ZANU high command were all Shona Karanga tribesmen who joined ZAPU much earlier in the war, before splitting to form ZANU. The KoreKore and Zezuru resented what they saw as Karanga tribal monopoly of ZANLA's key leadership.

6. Smith, 174-5. Years later, the Rhodesian CIO chief, Ken Flower, would reveal that Chitepo's assassination was a CIO operation, which happened to be timed perfectly to coincide with existing ZANU discord. Everyone in Zambia, including the Zambian government, believed Tongogara assassinated Chitepo. Chitepo's death would lead to more infighting in ZANU.

7. Martin, 159-167, 179.

8. Moorcraft, 41.

9. Moorcraft, 41-2.

10. CF20110920H001, former RAR officer, interview by author; Wood, *War Diaries*, 12. As the officer interviewed indicated, the Rhodesian army's response to the government's lack of trust of black soldiers was "absolute rubbish."

11. Owen, 2-3; Banda, *Saints*, 20; James Dobbins et al., *The UN's Role in Nation-Building: From the Congo to Iraq* (Santa Monica, CA: RAND, 2005), 5.

12. Wood, "Chimurenga," 199.

13. Major Dennison rose to be a legend within the Rhodesian Army. Born in Bradford, England, he served in the British Army in several regiments, including 22 SAS in Borneo. He was seconded to the Malaysian Rangers from 1965-68, to the Malawi Rifles from 1969-71 and retired from the British Army in 1975 to accept a three year commission with the Rhodesian Army. Enroute to Rhodesia, Dennison stumbled across a mercenary ring forming up to attack Rhodesia from Zambia. When he notified the Director of Military Intelligence, Lt. Col. Peter Hosking (later the CO, 2RAR), Hosking agreed he should join the group and act as an informant. During a party for the mercenary group on the eve of their departure for Lusaka, the group drew too much attention to itself and lost its sponsor. The group dispersed, and on 1 October 1975, Dennison joined 2RAR to command A Company. He was a no-nonsense leader

and an outstanding Fireforce commander, "who inspired his men by example, professionalism and dedication to defending the hard-pressed people of all race groups in Rhodesia." Andre Dennison was killed on 3 June 1979 by friendly fire. Wood, *War Diaries*, viii, 5.

14. CE20110910H0001, former RAR officer, interview.

15. CE20110909T0001, former RAR officer, interview.

16. Moorcraft, 42; Wood, *War Diaries*, 51. In May 1976, national service was extended from 12 to 18 months, and national servicemen in the field due to stand down were retained on active service. Territorial forces (comprised of national servicemen) were kept in the field. This trend would continue as the tempo of the war continued to increase and whites began to leave the country in larger numbers.

17. Binda, *Masodja*, 284-94; Moorcraft, 41-3; Binda, *Saints*, 185.

18. Wood, *Counterstrike*, 43-4; Desfountain, paragraph 7.

19. CE20110910H0001, former RAR officer, interview.

20. CE20110910W0001, former RR NCO, interview by author, Durban, Republic of South Africa, 10 September 2011.

21. CE20110910W0001.

22. Cilliers, 172-5.

23. Reid-Daly, *Top Secret War*, 338; J. R. T. Wood, "Counter-punching on the Mudzi: D Company, 1st Rhodesian African Rifles, on operation 'Mardon' 1 November 1976," *Small Wars and Insurgencies* 9, no. 2 (Autumn 1998): 64.

24. Reid-Daly, *Top Secret War,* 321-406. In August 1976, Operation Eland, a flying column of Selous Scouts, with 14 vehicles and 84 troops, armed with vehicle mounted 20mm cannons (taken from scrapped Vampire fighters), twin MAG machine guns, 12.7mm anti-aircraft guns, twin .30 caliber Browning machine guns, and 81mm mortars drove 30 km into Mozambique to a ZANLA training base on the Nyadzonya River known to contain over 5,000 insurgents. The Scouts arrived on the camp wearing FRELIMO uniforms just after ZANLA's morning parade-as planned-and opened fire, killing between 1,000 and 1,300 insurgents before driving back across the border to Rhodesia. Captured documents and insurgents from the raid clearly indicated the purpose and intent of this camp as a training facility for ZANLA, but ZANU and FRELIMO, as was to be the standard, insisted that Rhodesians were murdering civilians in refugee camps.

25. Wood, *Small Wars,* 69-72.

26. Wood, *Small Wars,* 74-81; CE20110913M0001, former RAR officer, interview; CE20110909T0001, former RAR officer, interview.

27. Binda, *Masodja*, 372-4; Cilliers, 197; CE20110913M0001, former RAR officer, interview; CE20110909T0001, former RAR officer, interview.

28. CE20110910H0001, former RAR officer, interview; Peter J. Hosking, foreward to *The War Diaries of André Dennison,* by J. R. T. Wood (Gibraltar: Ashanti, 1989), viii-ix.

29. CE20110913M0001, former RAR officer, interview. The RAR soldiers' strengths on OP missions are also documented in Binda, *Masodja,* 310-11.

30. Binda, *Masodja,* 311.

31. Binda, 295.

32. Smith, 198-9. Shuttle diplomacy is the use of a third party to resolve a diplomatic crisis, in this case the introduction of the United States as an intermediary between Britain and Rhodesia. Kissinger used this technique most famously in the 1973 negotiation of the cessation of hostilities after the Yom Kippur War between Israel and the Arab states led by Egypt and Syria. Kissinger's technique was to isolate each party, extract demands and possible concessions, and shuttle between the two until a compromise was accepted by both parties. The Rhodesian situation was complicated by the fact that although Britain was not a belligerent party, they were legally required to endorse any compromise government in order for Rhodesia to gain international recognition and for sanctions to be lifted. As such, Kissinger treated the black nationalist groups (ZANU, ZAPU and ANC), and the leaders of the frontline states, as a third leg of the agreement.

33. In April 1975, the People's Army of Vietnam forces entered Saigon, destroying the US backed government of the Republic of Vietnam and creating a unified communist state. This came after the US withdrew all troops and support for Vietnam, and was widely viewed as a strategic failure of the United States in stopping the spread of communism. Also in 1975, the US was further embarrassed by its involvement in backing the FPLA in Angola against Cuban and Russian communist-backed MPLA. The MPLA soundly defeated the FPLA, and the US was smeared with a second consecutive foreign policy debacle. For more on the US in Vietnam, see John Nagl, Dale Andrade, or Richard Hunt's works. For more on Angola, see Fred Bridgland or John Cann's works.

34. Stephen S. Rosenfeld, "Henry Kissinger on the USand Rhodesia," *Washington Post,* 3 July 1979.

35. Smith, 189.

36. Smith, 202-222.

37. Wood, *War Diaries,* 60. "[D]uring the first half of 1976 Rhodesia had endured a net loss of 2,271 whites, compared with a net gain of 1,590 whites in the first half of 1975.

38. Smith, 223.

Chapter 6
Phase Four: 1977-1979

During phase four, from 1977-79, the Rhodesian government began to genuinely move towards majority rule, with negotiations beginning in late 1977 and ending with the March 1978 Internal Settlement. Bishop Abel Muzorewa, Ian Smith, Ndabaningi Sithole and Chief Jeremiah Chirau formed an interim government with an eye toward a popular election and a path to increased black participation in the political process. ZANU and ZAPU formed the Patriotic Front coalition and refused to participate in this process, but remained aligned against each other and in separate camps in Mozambique and Zambia as they stepped up attacks in Rhodesia. Rhodesian military actions focused on external strikes at the core of ZANLA's and ZIPRA's support structures in Mozambique and Zambia, while political militias and "turned insurgents" formed into Security Force Auxiliaries to provide security in tribal areas.[1]

There were also some significant changes to the RAR during this period. The first black officers were commissioned in June 1977, and with the advent of majority rule following the Internal Settlement, national service was extended to the blacks, bringing in the first black conscripts into the Rhodesia Regiment and the RAR.

Internal Settlement

After the failed conference in Geneva, Ian Smith believed that continued reliance on Great Britain, South Africa and the United States to solve the Rhodesian problem was futile. The disparate and constantly fluctuating agenda of outside influences were not constructive in finding any meaningful solution, nor was it truly in their interests to do so. "We all came to the conclusion that our salvation lay in working together with our internal black leaders-in spite of their shortcomings they seemed more reliable than our so-called 'friends' of the free world."[2]

So in late 1977, Smith met with moderate black leaders to work on a settlement. Smith's objective was to determine and agree upon a way to implement the Anglo-American Agreement presented by Kissinger in 1976. Participating black leaders were "Muzorewa, Gabellah (from Matabeleland), Chikerema, Ndabaningi Sithole, and the two chiefs, Chirau and Kayisa Ndweni."[3]

As Ian Smith explained in his New Year's Message to Rhodesia on 31 December 1977:

The British have been trying to settle the Rhodesian problem in a manner which would best settle their own interests, rather than the interests of Rhodesia. Rhodesians have thus come to the conclusion that their best bet is to bring Rhodesians together around the settlement table, to the exclusion of outside interference. The talks are proceeding well and I believe all delegations will agree that we have made significant progress. The basic position remains the same. In exchange for acceptance of the principle of majority rule, we are negotiating the inclusion in the constitution of those safeguards necessary to retain the confidence of our white people, so that they will be encouraged to go on living and working in Rhodesia and thus continue to make their contribution to the economic progress of the country.[4]

The settlement discussions continued from January through March, making slow progress towards a final agreement. Both Joshua Nkomo and Robert Mugabe were absent from these discussions, having elected instead to meet as the newly formed "Patriotic Front" (PF)[5] with the new British Foreign Secretary (David Owen) and the new American Ambassador to the UN (Andrew Young) in Malta.

The Malta Conference resulted in the Patriotic Front accepting a UN role in supervising elections, and called for a ten man Governing Council made up of two representatives from each of the delegations in Geneva (Mugabe, Sithole, Nkomo, Muzorewa, and Smith) and a Resident Commissioner, presumably British. Additionally, and particularly objectionable to Smith, was a requirement that the Chief Justice, Police Commissioner and Secretary to the Cabinet vacate their posts, presumably the first of many required to do so. Not only did Smith reject the outcomes of Malta and a follow up conference (called "Malta Two") held in Dar es Salaam, but David Owen and US Secretary of State Chris Vance-the hosts of Malta Two-agreed that the PF's insistence on dominating any settlement was "unacceptable."[6]

The results of the Rhodesian government's meetings from January to March 1978, however, ended in a signed agreement among all participants (Smith, Muzorewa, Sithole, and Chirau) on 4 March 1978. The resulting interim government, run by an Executive Council of the four signatories, was tasked to "organize a cease-fire, to remove racial discrimination, to draft a new constitution and to hold elections later in the year before a handover to 'black' government at the end of December."[7] Smith negotiated an assurance that the white minority retained a voice by securing 28 seats of 100 in parliament and requiring a three-quarters majority to enact any constitutional change. Nkomo and Mugabe completely rejected the Internal Settlement because the military and police remained under white control, and they objected to whites retaining a blocking minority in the parliament.[8]

The interim government, as designed in the Internal Settlement, went into effect and proceeded to undertake the immense tasks before it. The most immediate challenge facing the interim government under Muzorewa- and perhaps the most difficult-was the actual achievement of a cease fire. The Patriotic Front, staunchly opposed to any progress that did not grant its ringleaders immediate and uncompromised personal power, set out to prevent any semblance of progress by Muzorewa and Smith's government. The three black signatories to the Internal Settlement were dubbed the "blacksmiths," and ZANLA declared 1978 "the Year of the People," to be filled with preparations for *Gore re Gukurahundi*, or the "Year of the People's Storm," in 1979. By mid-1978, ZANLA had infiltrated 13,000 guerrillas into Rhodesia, spread across the country and training local forces to support the insurgency.[9]

For its part, ZIPRA also escalated the war, attempting to discredit the Interim Transitional Government. On 3 September 1978, ZIPRA insurgents shot down an Air Rhodesia civilian aircraft with a SAM-7 missile as it was taking off from Lake Kariba with 52 passengers aboard. Horrific stories later emerged of ZIPRA guerrillas murdering the survivors of this attack, and public revulsion of Nkomo and ZIPRA was palpable. A second attack on an Air Rhodesia aircraft in February 1979 killed 59 civilians, and further cemented hatred for ZIPRA among Rhodesian whites and security forces.[10]

"The Spear of the People:" Security Force Auxiliaries

In bringing about a ceasefire between the government and the vast network of insurgents in the country, the Executive Council believed that Muzorewa's ANC (now called United African National Council, or UANC) and Sithole's faction of ZANU[11] could bring their followers over to the government side. With majority rule achieved, the government assumed that the insurgents would have no more reason to fight. Both Muzorewa and Sithole claimed to be in control of the majority of ZANLA forces, and each duly called for their "armies" to switch sides and become auxiliaries to RSF. Called the "Spear of the People"-*Pfomu re Vanhu* in Chishona, or *Umkonto wa Bantu* in Sindebele-the Security Force Auxiliaries (SFAs) were hastily established to feed, clothe, train, and pay turned insurgents who accepted the offer to fight for the Interim Transitional Government.[12]

The real problem was the loyalty of the SFAs to their respective political factions rather than to Rhodesia itself. Whereas the RAR-indeed, all of the RSF-were staunchly apolitical,[13] the SFAs were defined as political forces. In this respect, they were similar to ZANU and ZAPU. Training these men was a difficult process, as they did not believe they had anything to learn from the RSF. Once employed, they worked in tribal areas, and Security Forces were not allowed into those areas. In effect, the SFAs were allowed to operate like ZANLA or ZIPRA and feed off the population, as long as they did so in the name of the Interim Transitional Government rather than ZANU or ZAPU.[14]

In practice, the SFA program was a failure. Neither Muzorewa nor Sithole had a solid connection to the actual ZANLA forces in Rhodesia. The vast majority of Muzorewa's and Sithole's followers who turned out for SFA training had never been insurgents-most were rounded up by UANC and ZANU(Sithole) from the villages in order to add to the numbers of each faction's "army." Training for the SFAs was initially the job of the Selous Scouts. As Reid-Daly notes, "[n]either my officers nor I viewed the new order of things with any marked enthusiasm, because none of us could see it working, but orders were orders, so the Selous Scouts swung into disciplined action." The selection of Selous Scouts to train former insurgents to fight for the interim government was an interesting choice. If any actual ZANLA insurgents ever discovered their trainers were the hated *sku'zapo*,[15] this would surely introduce unnecessary tension into the situation. But, as most of the new trainees had never actually been insurgents, and the Scouts were very careful not to reveal their identity, it never became a problem.[16]

Needless to say, the real ZANLA took some exception to the SFAs. In at least one instance, a recently trained group of Muzorewa's SFAs were moving into the Wedza TTL to establish themselves, only to be captured by a ZANLA group operating there. The ZANLA group stumbled upon a few newly trained SFA soldiers who had separated from the group, and quickly ordered two of them to return to the main SFA group and arrange a meeting. The inexperienced auxiliaries agreed, and were promptly taken prisoner by ZANLA. Most of these auxiliaries were summarily executed. Forty-one corpses were later discovered by a Police Reserve Air Wing pilot overflying the area. The few who escaped reported back to police what had happened. The Scouts quickly made contact with the ZANLA group and within a week killed 29 of them, either directly or by calling in fireforce.[17]

The RAR took over training the SFAs in August 1979. As with the Scouts, the RAR were not enthusiastic about the mission, but they carried out their orders. In recalling the SFA training program, one former RAR officer stated that he (a Lieutenant at the time) and his CSM were called aside, given a task to develop and execute a six-week training program for the *phomu re vanhu*. Unsure exactly what the program was or why they were involved, the Lieutenant and NCO duly executed a very basic training program, consisting of marksmanship and fundamental military skills before passing out their trainees less than two months later.[18]

RAR Actions

Much of the RAR's activity during this phase was fireforce action and night patrols. A typical fireforce call-up, involving A Company 2RAR, occurred on 9 October 1978, when a Selous Scouts OP in Operation Area Repulse reported 50 insurgents between the Lundi River and a smaller tributary.[19]

A Lynx aircraft initiated contact, marking the target for a strike by Hunter fighter-bombers of the RhAF. Following this bomb run, the K-Car carrying the company commander, Maj André Dennison, arrived overhead. Two "stop groups" were inserted by helicopter (G-Cars) along likely avenues of escape, while four sticks of paratroopers jumped in to form a sweep line and flush out the insurgents. In the ensuing firefight, the troops on the ground, guided by Dennison and the K-Car pilot, conducted multiple sweeps, displaying aggressive and thorough pursuit of the enemy. In the end, up to 38 insurgents and trainees were killed, one insurgent was captured, and six escaped. Because only 16 weapons were found, however, SB only credited the fireforce with 16 kills. Dennison disputed this claim- according to him, the target was a training camp, so not all the trainees were armed but most had webbing and several had hand grenades. While directing the action from the K-Car, Maj Dennison was shot through his knee but remained overhead for another hour and fifteen minutes until the K-Car had to refuel. Dennison and the sweep group commander, WOII Mandava Dick, were later recommended for the Bronze Cross of Rhodesia for their actions that day.[20]

At dusk on 11 August 1978, an eight-man patrol from Support Company 1RAR, led by Lieutenant Pat Lawless, was operating in the Devil's Gorge area of Zambia[21] in conjunction with a simultaneous SAS operation. Lawless' patrol made contact with three insurgents, killing two and fatally wounding the other. As the wounded man was dying, Lawless interrogated him and learned of a nearby insurgent company of about 100 men:

Lawless laid an ambush for the night-he had two MAGs. He also set up a claymore mine along the track but nothing happened. However, at first light, as they began to dismantle the claymore, preparatory to moving on, they saw some 70 insurgents approaching along the track. Every soldier immediately squirmed back into his position and waited for Lawless to spring the ambush. As soon as the enemy was in the killing ground, the order was given. Eight insurgents were killed and 15 wounded in this initial attack. A further 20 men, initially unseen, tried to outflank the patrol by sneaking down the hillock behind their position. However, Corporal Ernest Rashmira noted the move and, leaping up, charged them, firing bursts from his MAG, killing three.[22]

After continuing the attack for several hours against such overwhelming odds, the small patrol, low on ammunition, withdrew. Lawless was later awarded the Silver Cross of Rhodesia for this and other actions.[23]

In many instances similar to the two described above, the RAR continued to demonstrate their ability to engage and destroy their enemy. The lessons from early operations like Nickel and Cauldron were well-learned and the regiment was emerging as a superb counterinsurgent force. Recruiting continued and young black Rhodesians volunteered in droves to join the RAR as operations continued across the country (and beyond).

Changes to the RAR

As early as the breakup of the federation, the Rhodesian Army had begun to consider commissioning black officers for service in the regiment. In the early 1970s, one former RAR officer recalls evaluating a number of black candidates for selection to the Cadet Course at the School of Infantry in Gwelo. The Officer Selection Board was sufficiently impressed with the black candidate's attributes-after a five day selection course he was among the top five of twenty candidates. In the end, however, the Brigadier in charge of the board decided it was still too early to send one black cadet through the course by himself. As the RAR officer recalls, "it would be very unfair on the black chap to put him through the difficulties of integrating at the point in time when integration wasn't in the cards."[24]

In June 1977, however, the Rhodesian Army commissioned its first black officers. Two former RSMs-Martin Tumbare (RSM, 1RAR) and Wurayayi Mutero (RSM, 2RAR)-were commissioned, and more black officers followed. According to the Regimental History, "on 25 August, [Tumbare] was presented with the late 'Kim' Rule's sword by Mrs. Rule. It had been Kim Rule's wish that his sword be presented to the first African to be commissioned in the Rhodesia Army. Fittingly, it was a member of the battalion he had commanded who received the honour."[25]

Figure 1. Mrs. Rule, the widow of Lieutenant Colonel Kim Rule OBE, presents her late husband's sword to the first African to be commissioned, Lieutenant N. M. Tumbare DMM.

Source: Alexandre Binda, Masodja: The History of the Rhodesian African Rifles and its forerunner, the Rhodesia Native Regiment (Johannesburg: 30 Degrees South, 2007), 321.

Notes

1. Wood, *Counterstrike*, 44-6.
2. Smith, 237-8.
3. Smith, 242.
4. Smith, 241-2.
5. Formed in October 1976, the Patriotic Front (PF) was the latest attempt by the two nationalist parties-ZANU and ZAPU-to work together. The formation of the PF was a direct response to Nhongo and Mangena's formation of the ZIPA in January 1976, as well as an attempt to negotiate with the newly elected Democratic administration of the United States, and Labour Party government of Great Britain. Previous attempts at unifying ZANU and ZAPU, some mentioned in earlier chapters, were the Joint Military Command (JMC) formed in February 1972, the Front for the Liberation of Zimbabwe (FROLIZI), formed in October 1974, the unification of ZANU, ZAPU and FROLIZI under Muzorewa's ANC in December 1974, and finally the uniting of elements of ZANLA and ZIPRA to form ZIPA in January 1976. Every attempt was brought about due to outside pressure, and each ended in failure. In fact, by the end of the war, ZIPRA and ZANLA were fighting each other in Rhodesia when they weren't fighting the RSF. For an excellent discussion on Zimbabwean attempts at unity, see Daniel R. Kempton, *Soviet Strategy Toward Southern Africa* (New York: Praeger, 1989), 118-125.
6. Smith, 252.
7. Martin, 293.
8. Martin.
9. Martin, 292.
10. Binda, *Masodja*, 327, 364; CE20110913M0001, former RAR officer, interview.
11. Sithole never really relinquished leadership of ZANU after he was deposed by Robert Mugabe. The resulting split in ZANU meant that a small faction remained loyal to Sithole and operated inside Rhodesia while the vast majority of the movement was controlled by Mugabe from Mozambique. The smaller group is commonly referred to as ZANU (Sithole). Reid-Daly, *Top Secret War*, 564.
12. Reid-Daly, *Top Secret War*, 563-5.
13. CE20110913M0001, former RAR officer, interview.
14. Reid-Daly, *Top Secret War*, 567.
15. Reid-Daly, *Top Secret War*, 146. *Sku'zapo* was the nickname used by the insurgents to describe the Selous Scouts. According to Reid-Daly, "'*Skuz*,' is a corruption of the English, *excuse me*, while *apo* is the Shona word for *here* in the immediate sense. Thus, in direct translation *Skuz'apo* might mean: *Excuse*

me here . . . or: *excuse me for what I have just done.*" In context, it refers to the way two pickpockets approach their victim, one bumping the target and muttering "*skuz'apo*" while the other takes advantage of the distraction to lift his wallet. The Selous Scouts took great pride in their nickname, and their distinct unpopularity among the enemy.

16. Reid-Daly, 565-6; CB20111110S0001, former Selous Scout officer, interview. No clear reason is evident for the selection of the Selous Scouts as the training force for the SFAs. Reid-Daly suggests that by this point his force had become a "go-to" force for nearly any unsolveable problem-indeed, that may be true. Or perhaps, as one former Scout officer proposed, their status as former insurgents may have helped in understanding the minds of their new trainees. And as hated as the Scouts were, they certainly commanded the respect of the insurgents. The SFA training mission would pass to the RAR in 1979.

17. Reid-Daly, *Top Secret War*, 570-1.

18. CG20110927S0001, former RAR officer, interview.

19. Binda, *Masodja*, 344-5; Wood, *War Diaries*, 273-5.

20. Binda, *Masodja*, 344-5; Wood, *War Diaries*, 273-5.

21. The RAR did conduct external operations, like the one described here, into Zambia and Mozambique. These patrols routinely submitted false Location Station (LOCSTAT) reports to prevent enemy knowledge of their operations.

22. Binda, *Masodja*, 349.

23. Binda.

24. CE20110909R0001, former RAR officer, interview. The candidate in question commissioned into the Corps of Signals in 1978. He rose to the rank of Captain before the end of the war, and was believed to have retired from the Zimbabwe Army years later as a Lieutenant Colonel.

25. Binda, *Masodja*, 315. Lt. Col. G. E. L. "Kim" Rule commanded 1RAR from 1950-1955. While he was CO, Rule was responsible for the regiment receiving its colors from the Queen. His manuscript of the history of the regiment was a critical primary source for the writers of *Masodja*.

Chapter 7
Phase Five: April 1979-April 1981

> On 30 January 1979, the (white) Rhodesian electorate went to the polls in a referendum on the majority-rule constitution. An overwhelming 85% voted 'yes' to black rule-probably one of the few times in history a people have willingly and deliberately voted themselves out of power. However, the British government declared the result irrelevant.
>
> —Alexandre Binda, *Masodja: the History of the Rhodesian African Rifles and its Forerunner, the Rhodesia Native Regiment*

During the final phase of the war, Rhodesia voted itself into majority rule under its first black Prime Minister. Under the new government, and now called Zimbabwe-Rhodesia, the nation expected recognition from the British as well as an end to sanctions, having met all six conditions for recognition as laid out by the British government in 1965-6. However, ZANU and ZAPU refused to accept the arrangement, and instead intensified their military actions. The British declared the 1979 elections irrelevant, and the UN continued sanctions. In September 1979, the British hosted a conference in London, at Lancaster House, between the government of Zimbabwe-Rhodesia and the PF, along with representatives of the frontline states. In the subsequent election, Robert Mugabe and ZANU(PF) were voted into power. Zimbabwe was granted independence on 18 April 1980.[1]

The Army during this phase fought desperately to suppress ZANLA insurgents flooding the country, while striking at external targets in Zambia and Mozambique. The Third Battalion of RAR formed in October 1979, consolidating several of the racially integrated Independent Companies of the Rhodesia Regiment under one headquarters. Once Mugabe took control of the country, the former RSF organizations began to break apart, and many of the white soldiers and officers chose to resign and leave the country.

The RAR, however, remained intact and began to integrate with its erstwhile enemies, ZANLA and ZIPRA. In large holding camps across the country, ZANLA and ZIPRA consolidated alongside each other and frequently clashed, most notably at a camp outside Bulawayo called Entumbane. Here, the RAR stood between ZIPRA and ZANLA to prevent the wholesale slaughter of one by the other and protect the civilian population from the two warring factions.[2]

April 1979 Elections

1979 began with tremendous steps toward immediate majority rule in Rhodesia. The first step was a referendum among the white population to accept the majority rule constitution as drafted by the Interim Transition Government of Muzorewa, Smith, Sithole and Chirau. Placing their faith in the "black moderates," the white population of Rhodesia overwhelmingly voted in favor of black rule in their country. Subsequently, on from 17-20 April, nearly 2 million black voters-about 64 percent of the country's eligible voters-went to the polls, and on the principal of "one man, one vote," elected Bishop Muzorewa's UANC into power, under the "Government of National Unity" between the various parties. This was a historic undertaking, and one which Rhodesians hoped would end the war. Several teams of international observers, including a British team led by Lord Boyd, reported that the elections were free and fair, by the strictest Western standards.[3]

From April to August 1979, Rhodesians waited for the Carter administration in the United States and the newly elected Conservative government of Margaret Thatcher in Britain to recognize Zimbabwe-Rhodesia. As the US and Britain delayed recognition of the new government, ZANLA and ZIPRA increased their operations, further taxing an already extremely stressed RSF.[4] From late 1978 to May 1979, officially recorded monthly incidents nearly tripled, from under 600 to 1,706 as insurgent groups, primarily ZANLA, exacted revenge for local support given to the UANC. "By September 1979, the UANC popular base had vanished."[5]

Finally, instead of recognizing the new Zimbabwe-Rhodesia Government of National Unity, "on Monday, 6 August, at the Commonwealth conference in Lusaka, Margaret Thatcher reneged on her promise of recognition under pressure from Nigeria and Australia and set another course with a new commitment to an all-party conference in London."[6] This conference brought Nkomo and Mugabe back to the table with the Zimbabwe-Rhodesia government. In advising Muzorewa on attending the conference, Smith says:

> [W]hile I had previously resisted any thought of an all-party conference, believing that if we persisted we would gain recognition of our honest and straightforward effort, I was reconciling myself to a change of thought, and my close colleagues in the Rhodesian Front agreed. There were two main reasons I have mentioned. First, the terrorists were gaining support among the indigenous

population, not through convincing argument an appeal, but by using the dreadful weapon of intimidation. Second, the Western leaders would not face up to making a decision which conflicted with the views of the OAU-90 per cent of whose membership comprised countries governed by communist leaders.[7]

In September 1979, the British Foreign Secretary, Lord Peter Carrington, hosted a constitutional conference at Lancaster House in London. All parties, including Mugabe and Nkomo, were to resolve the problem of majority rule in Rhodesia.

Lancaster House Conference

From 10 September to 23 December 1979, delegations led by Ian Smith, Robert Mugabe, Joshua Nkomo, and Abel Muzorewa attended the Lancaster House conference, along with delegations from the frontline states. The purpose of the conference was to develop an acceptable framework for the government and set a date for internationally supervised elections. Carrington's approach to settling the problem differed from previous attempts. Rather than negotiate primarily with the PF, his proposals "first were directed at Mozambique and Zambia as the countries serving as hosts to the insurgents. Both countries were economically desperate for an end to a war that was threatening to engulf them."[8] In fact, without pressure from Samora Machel of Mozambique, Mugabe would have left the conference and forfeited his stake in the British negotiations entirely.[9]

The results of the Lancaster House Conference were agreements to an immediate ceasefire, a Commonwealth monitoring force under General John Acland to supervise movement of belligerents into 16 assembly points, and an election to be held as soon as possible.

RAR Actions

Fireforce actions continued, at an increasing pace for the RAR. In Operation Area Hurricane during November 1979, Support Company 1RAR planned an attack on a "liberated area" in a Tribal Trust Land, from which insurgents were routinely shooting at a Police Reserve Air Wing (PRAW) light aircraft. According to the plan, the PRAW pilot was to fly his normal route, with a 1RAR fireforce following about 15 miles behind. If the plane drew fire, the pilot was to drop a smoke marker on his way out of the area, and the fireforce would arrive directly behind to deal with the insurgents. The fireforce consisted of two K-Cars, four G-Cars (each with a four-man stop group), with a reserve of paratroops standing by at the airfield. There was also a land tail carrying more troops, ammunition and heavy weapons, driving a specific route to assist in any contact.[10]

On the morning of 14 November, the PRAW aircraft duly took off on his route, and the fireforce and land tail were shortly behind, following a preset pattern of rendezvous points while the helicopters flew just above the ground to avoid detection. At one such rendezvous point, the Company Sergeant Major (leading the land tail) reported spotting a group of 30 insurgents running into the hills 3 kilometers away. The fireforce immediately turned and deployed to engage the insurgents, with the K-Cars firing their 20mm cannon at the fleeing men. Shortly after a Lynx dropped a frantan[11] canister near the top of a prominent *dwala,*[12] the stop groups on G-Cars landed at the top. After receiving reinforcements flown in from the land tail, two sticks formed a sweep line and moved out to establish contact with the insurgents, now estimated at a strength of 40-50 men and hiding in a riverbed. The fireforce commander decided to use helicopters to cover the far exits of the riverbed as the sweep groups advanced.[13]

After advancing about thirty meters into their sweep, the RAR soldiers came under heavy fire, and remained in contact with this group of insurgents for the rest of the day and into the night, receiving reinforcements from the land tail through the afternoon. At one point, the commander of the first wave of troops, Lt. Lawless:

> Pulled my stop groups back from the cave, and called in an air strike from a Canberra armed with 200 Alpha bombs (small football shaped bombs which bounced, armed, then detonated at about waist-height), which had been scrambled from Salisbury and was orbiting the contact area. The first box of 50 bombs fell well short, the second landed beyond the target-and the third landed on my sweep line! Miraculously, nobody was hurt, and the Canberra pilot, obviously embarrassed by his performance so far, made no mistake with the fourth box, which landed short and bounced into the cave, shredding the luckless terrs inside.[14]

The RAR troops maintained contact through the night, engaging insurgents attempting to escape. In the morning, Lieutenant Lawless says, "I reported to my commanding officer that we had killed 26 terrs for the loss of one officer killed [Captain Jim Hardy, shot in the head during the initial sweep] and one wounded, and handed over command to him. By 1000, we were back at Mtoko [the fireforce base] . . . and by 1130 we were once again airborne en route to another terrorist sighting."[15]

Operation Murex

Shortly after this fireforce action, in November 1979, Support Company 1RAR was selected for an external operation into Zambia. Selous Scouts had discovered and frustrated ZIPRA plans for a conventional invasion of Rhodesia. During operations in Zambia, Lieutenant Edwin (Piringondo) of Selous Scouts discovered, mapped, and conducted reconnaissance on a ZIPRA brigade in a fortified base in the Kabanga Mission area (about 80 miles northeast of Livingstone). Support Company 1RAR and a troop of Selous Scouts were to attack the base and, if possible, capture the radios and message pads to decipher coded messages from a ZIPRA team operating in Rhodesia. The attack was coordinated to start at 1230 on the designated day, because at that time, ZIPRA soldiers were typically all cleaning their weapons.[16]

After detailed planning and rehearsals and one-day weather delay, the operation was a "go," and it went "like clockwork." Seven Hunters, three Canberras and four K-Cars conducted preliminary air strikes, while two G-Cars, four Cheetahs,[17] and the Paradak all delivered troops to their objectives on time, receiving almost no ground-fire (because all of ZIPRA's weapons were disassembled for cleaning) in the process.

After a short sharp contact with a few determined members of ZIPRA, we found and captured the radios and codes, which were immediately airlifted out by a Cheetah. A number of well-sited bunkers were located under trees among anthills, but the paras re-assembled ZIPRA's AA weapons (heavy Soviet 12.7 and 14.5mm machine guns) and blasted them. We found large food and ammunition supplies, which took several hours to clear. We killed 35 members of ZIPRA and captured five for the loss of one Selous Scout killed. One trooper and a pilot were injured by ground-fire while over-flying another large and hitherto unsuspected ZIPRA position as we withdrew.[18]

A few weeks later, the Rhodesian Army forces would withdraw back within its own borders as Lord Soames, the interim British governor, arrived to facilitate the peace settlement negotiated at Lancaster House.

The RAR in 1979 was busily engaged as a highly effective counterinsurgent force. Again, by this stage they were deployed constantly against ever-increasing numbers of ZANLA and ZIPRA, but they never wavered in their commitment, nor was recruiting a challenge. The soldiers remained absolutely loyal to the regiment, and the regiment remained true to the country.

3RAR forms

In September 1979, Army Headquarters announced that several of the independent companies of the Rhodesia Regiment, now teeming with conscripted black national servicemen, would form the Third Battalion RAR. Two independent companies based in Umtali in eastern Rhodesia-along with a third independent company in nearby Inyanga-rebadged into the RAR. These companies had served with some distinction alongside the RAR and RLI in recent years, and they were well respected by both regiments. Senior NCOs from 1RAR and 2RAR came to the new battalion, and Depot RAR in Balla Balla ran several courses "to inculcate the values and traditions required of RAR soldiers into the Umtali and Inyanga troops."[19]

Lieutenant Colonel Terry Leaver was the first commander of the battalion, and by October 1979, 3RAR commenced operations. By this time, the Lancaster House Conference was ongoing, and the battalion's first missions were to prevent ZANLA infiltration across the Mozambique border during the conference. The battalion continued to operate on the eastern border throughout the transition of government. In March 1981, 3RAR would be designated 33 Infantry Battalion of the Zimbabwe Army under the command of Lieutenant Colonel Ron Marillier.[20]

Mugabe Elected

By 6 January 1980, Lt. Gen. Acland's Commonwealth Monitoring Force-about 1,300 strong-had assembled 15,730 insurgents in assembly points. Within days, the number grew to 22,000, of which 16,500 were ZANLA and the remainder ZIPRA. RSF were restricted to their bases until elections were complete. Importantly, thousands of insurgents did not report to the Assembly Points; among these were the political commissars, key leaders, and "hard-core insurgents." Most of the population of the Assembly Point camps was *mujiba*, (local informants) and low-level recruits. Left among the population, the "hard-cores" would continue to intimidate and coerce the people to vote their way-for Mugabe.[21]

On 4 March 1980, the election results revealed that Mugabe had won 63 percent of the vote. On 18 April, he became the Prime Minister of an independent Zimbabwe, as Prince Charles and Lord Soames handed over the country and departed. 1RAR provided the guard of honor for the farewell ceremony.[22]

The RAR in the Zimbabwe Army

The three battalions of RAR continued to serve in the Zimbabwe Army, along with many of its officers. The three battalions of the regiment were designated 11, 22, and 33 Infantry Battalions of the Zimbabwe Army. While the rest of the army struggled to integrate factions of ZIPRA, ZANLA, and Rhodesian forces, the RAR remained as it was, and provided a model professional force for its sister units in the Zimbabwe Army.[23]

Other elements of the Rhodesian Army, however, did not survive the transition to Zimbabwe. The RLI disbanded on 17 October 1980. The SAS disbanded 31 December 1980. The Selous Scouts were integrated back into their parent regiments, and those who had only ever been Scouts consolidated into 4th (Holding Unit) RAR. "On 1 October 1980, 4 (HU) RAR ended its short life and became the 1st Zimbabwe Parachute Battalion." Many of the officers and men of the RLI, SAS, and even a few from the RAR went to South Africa and served in the South African Defense Force (SADF). In fact, a Pathfinder Company of SADF's 44 Paras, called "The Philistines," was made up entirely of ex-Rhodesians.[24]

For some time, the RAR remained untouched, retaining its distinctive badge, uniform, and shoulder patch (minus a "Rhodesia" insignia). In correspondence, the Battalion Commnader, Lt Col. Mick McKenna, continued to refer to his unit as "11 Infantry Battalion (1RAR)." The commanders and many officers continued to serve with the same men they had trained and fought beside throughout the war. There was some hope that this would remain so, and that the new Zimbabwe could form a professional force and transition into the peaceful, integrated society that had been the objective for so long.[25]

Entumbane: "The Battle for Bulawayo"

The first Zimbabwe government was an uneasy union, under Prime Minister Robert Mugabe, of three factions-Mugabe's ZANU, Nkomo's ZAPU, and Smith's Rhodesian Front (in a much smaller capacity than before). The armies of these three factions were billeted together at various assembly points across the country as they waited for integration into the new national army. Old rivalries between ZANLA and ZIPRA dominated the camps, leading to several tense situations. The political and military situation was not helped by constant ZANU(PF) propaganda distributed throughout the country, over television and radio broadcasts. The situation deteriorated rapidly when the newly appointed ZANU(PF) Minister of Finance, Mr. Enos Nkala, made a pair of speeches in November 1980 emphasizing the creation of a one-party state under the leadership of ZANU(PF).[26]

In response to Nkala's rhetoric and ZANU(PF) propaganda, ZIPRA forces near the township of Entumbane just outside Bulawayo began to move truckloads of reinforcements into their camp. The ZANLA soldiers quartered there noticed the increase, and someone started shooting. Police riot squads were unable to contain the ensuing four hour firefight, which spread into the town. Small arms fire, rocket grenades, mortars and machine guns inspired civilian supporters in the town to join the fray, adding to the chaos.[27]

Zimbabwe Army command therefore ordered 1RAR (now designated 11 Infantry Battalion, Zimbabwe Army) to stop the fighting.

D Company was first on the scene and deployed along the railway line at Mpopoma, thus cutting off the city centre to the now-mutinous warring factions. Support Company was positioned on D Company's right flank. The Zimbabwe Army 12th Battalion was also in support but proved to be more of a hindrance than a help. During the afternoon, A, B, and C companies arrived and took up positions to the right of D Company and Support Company.[28]

At nightfall, the fighting subsided, but ZIPRA had called to their nearby Gwaai River Mine assembly point for heavy weapons and vehicles to support their fight. In the morning, the reinforced ZIPRA forces attacked ZANLA's position, and the RAR swung into action. As the RAR initiated their assault on ZIPRA and ZANLA under the cover of Hawker Hunter aircraft, the mutineers reconsidered their options and called for a ceasefire. Brigadier Mike Shute, commander of 1 Brigade Zimbabwe Army (and former commander of 1RAR), arranged for the mutineers to surrender their heavy weapons. 1RAR established an outpost at a beer hall overlooking the two camps, reinforced with mortars and a troop of armored cars to keep the peace. The battalion rotated a company at a time through observation duties at the beer hall in Entumbane.[29]

For the next few months, ZIPRA continued building strength in Matabeleland, apparently preparing for a coup. ZIPRA was concerned that they had no political future in Zimbabwe under Mugabe and ZANU(PF), and they had begun moving their vast stockpiles of Soviet equipment from Zambia into Zimbabwe. Equipped with T-34 tanks, armored cars, anti-aircraft guns, BTR-152 Armored Personnel Carriers, and about 6,000 soldiers, ZIPRA's forces were substantial. On 10 January, Mugabe fired Nkomo as Minister of Home Affairs. The RAR began planning for the imminent clash between ZIPRA and ZANLA.[30]

On 8 February, ZANLA soldiers attacked their ZIPRA colleagues in one of the assembly points, killing over 60 ZIPRA soldiers. When news of this incident reached the newly formed 13 Infantry Battalion-which was in training with a team of British instructors at another assembly point-the ZIPRA members of that battalion attacked their ZANLA colleagues, killing 12. Once again, D Company 1RAR arrived to restor order, and quickly drove into the camp to settle the issue. In the ensuing action, the RAR killed 40 ZIPRA soldiers, and much of the rest of the battalion was detained. "Arriving at work the following day, the British instructors were astonished to find the ZIPRA half of their trainees (minus the deceased and the escapees), clad only in underpants and squatting in neat silent rows under the watchful eyes of their RAR captors."[31]

The fighting continued over the next several days, during which a severely outnumbered 1RAR, reinforced with a troop of four armored cars[32] and supported by one Lynx aircraft, destroyed the better part of a motorized rifle battalion (equipped with Soviet BTR-152s). Of this action, the Lynx pilot explains:

> On the morning of the action [12 February 1981] I was dispatched as a first reaction singleton aircraft from the Thornhill base in Gwelo to Bulawayo to assist the RAR. . . . My aircraft was armed with the standard two machine guns and SNEB rockets, which, because we were expecting to be marking for the Hunters were only smoke, not HE. . . . [Once over the RAR's position] it was immediately apparent that he [Major Lionel Dyke] and his men were under considerable pressure and might be overrun. Lionel asked for a strike(s) on the position giving him the most problems. . . . I then put in a strike firing the SNEB as a distraction and strafing with machine guns. After pulling out from this I seem to remember that Lionel was most appreciative but did mention that all the fire directed at him was now concentrated on me; something along the lines of all hell let loose. He then asked me for another strike and it was during this attack that I took damage. I was in the dive when I took a number of rounds through the cockpit which took out the front engine, destroyed the right side of the instrument panel, passed an inch or so in front of my nose and then out of the left side of the aircraft. . . . I continued and strafed again but for lack of a front engine had to tell Lionel that I was off to Brady [airfield] but would be back as soon as I could. When I arrived I was greeted by a Wing Commander, who was a bit put out and it seemed to me at the time it was because I did not have the correct weapon load.[33]

According to the accounts in *Masodja*, when the commander of C Company 1RAR (Maj Lionel Dyke) called for air support, the request was denied. The pilot, however, heard the request, disobeyed orders and flew anyway, repeatedly striking targets in support of the RAR. His aircraft was repeatedly shot during his numerous gun and rocket runs. In *Masodja*, Maj. Dyke and Second Lieutenant John Hopkins (another officer involved the action) claim the pilot received or was recommended for a Silver Cross of Rhodesia. He did not receive any commendation, however, other than generous praise in subsequent correspondence between Dyke (1RAR), Brigadier Mike Shute (Commander, 1 Brigade), and Air Force Headquarters.[34]

On the evening of 12 February 1981, elements of the RAR battle group went to find the rest of ZIPRA's forces:

> The armoured cars were sent down to Essexvale battle camp to deal with ZIPRA's armoured battle group but soon found that the enemy was prepared to surrender their ten T34s and remaining BTR 152 APCs, GSP bridging equipment, artillery and amphibious vehicles. On inspection, it was found that the T34s were fortunately unserviceable. These captured vehicles were subsequently removed to the battalion's concentration area on Brady Barracks Airfield where the RAR removed souvenirs and useful items.[35]

The official casualty figures listed 260 dissident killed, but the RAR disagrees-the regiment accounted for over 400 dead on its own, without losing a man. After the Entumbane fight, massive ZIPRA factions deserted fearing retribution. Mugabe would never trust his Ndebele colleagues. He would eventually unleash a North Korean trained 5th Brigade of the Zimbabwe Army into Matabeleland in 1983 to massacre tens of thousands of Ndebele, accusing them of plotting against ZANU(PF).

The RAR's actions at Entumbane displayed-better than any other example-the loyalty and professional values of the regiment. By this point, everything had changed in Zimbabwe. The RAR's enemy had become its commander-in-chief. Its mission had gone from destroying two insurgent armies to integrating them. Outside of its own chain of command, the army around the RAR was a hollow shell of its former self. Lt. Gen. Walls stayed on briefly but had just resigned as the commander of the Zimbabwe Army, and nationalist faction leaders were filling the ranks of Army Headquarters. Fortunately, the headquarters of 1 Brigade, commanded by Brigadier (later Major General) Mike Shute remained largely intact, but the other units of the brigade and the army were beginning to degrade as a professional force-as 12 and 13 Infantry Battalions demonstrated during the actions in January and February 1981. 2RAR and 3RAR similarly remained intact, serving as model organizations within their respective brigades during similar ZANLA-ZIPRA confrontations in quieter areas of the country. Neither battalion had a large fight like 1RAR at Entumbane, however.[36]

So why would the RAR deliberately stop ZIPRA and ZANLA from killing each other? Why would white officers support the ZANU(PF) government, and why would black soldiers follow their white officers against black mutineers? As one officer involved in the fight said:

> My loyalties lay to my Brigade Commander (Mike Shute), my regiment, and to the country and its defenceless population. Insofar as the regiment was concerned, I believe their loyalty lay to their officers and, more importantly, to each other. . . . There were no instances of a reluctance to obey orders or desertion as we fought without fear or favour against both ZIPRA and ZANLA and anyone else who got in our way as we carried out our duties.[37]

The actions of the RAR at Entumbane saved Mugabe's government from certain civil war against an enemy (ZIPRA) that was heavily armed, trained and supported by Soviet backers. Indeed, many outside Rhodesia believed that either Nkomo's ZIPRA or Walls' former RSF forces would execute a *coup d'état* against Mugabe, but no coup ever materialized. The end result of Entumbane was a final blow to the military might of ZIPRA, and most of its Soviet equipment was captured and redistributed among the rest of the Zimbabwe Army.[38]

Conclusion

In the final phase of the Bush War, the RAR demonstrated its proficiency as a fighting force. The true nature of the loyalty and dedication of its soldiers to their regiment-never doubted during its history-was displayed one last time at Entumbane, where loyalty to anything else but the regiment would have faltered. The RAR by this point was an exemplary fighting force in its own right. The soldiers and leaders demonstrated tremendous learning and growth from Operation Nickel, where a company of RAR struggled against lightly armed, poorly trained insurgents in 1967, to Entumbane, where a battalion of RAR stood its ground against a motorized brigade, destroying a motorized battalion without losing a man.

Figure 1. RAR soldiers at Brady Barracks, February 1981.

Source: Alexandre Binda, Masodja: The History of the Rhodesian African Rifles and its forerunner, the Rhodesia Native Regiment (Johannesburg: 30 Degrees South, 2007).

In less than one year's time, the national government transitioned twice to majority rule-once to Bishop Muzorewa in April 1979, then to Robert Mugabe in March 1980. For the first time in its history, Rhodesia (as Zimbabwe-Rhodesia) pressed blacks into national service, leading to the formation of 3RAR and ending a long tradition of purely voluntary black service in the Rhodesian Army. Despite the tremendous pressure and volatile state of the country through its transition from Rhodesia to Zimbabwe, the RAR kept its tradition and culture alive and remained as a crucial element of stability in the new national army.

Notes

1. Binda, *Masodja*, 364, 383.

2. Binda, *Masodja*, 389.

3. Wood, *War Diaries*, 327-9. The vote was conducted at fixed and mobile polling stations across all eight electoral regions. Observed by a British Conservative Party team under Lord Boyd and several other international observers, 1,853,333 voters (63.9 percent of 2,900,000 eligible voters) went to the polls. Of these, 1,212,639 voted for Muzorewa's UANC (67.27 percent), 262,928 (14.58 percent) for Sithole's ZANU-PF, 194,446 (10.79 percent) for the United National Federal Party led by Chief Kayisa Ndiweni. Allocated by percentage of the vote, assembly seats awarded to each party were: 51 to UANC, 12 to ZANU-Sithole, and 9 seats to UNFP. The remaining 28 seats were reserved for the Rhodesian Front under Ian Smith to ensure that the sixth principal for recognition-that is, protection of the minority from the majority-was met.

4. Smith, 305-11.

5. Cilliers, 55.

6. Smith, 311; Wood, *War Diaries*, 355-8. Specifically, Nigeria nationalized British Petroleum holdings in its country and threatened further economic actions, including withdrawing from the Commonwealth, if Thatcher's government recognized Muzorewa's government and normalized relations with Zimbabwe-Rhodesia, as Thatcher stated she would do mere months before. Australian Prime Minister Malcolm Fraser supported Nigeria's action, as did Kenneth Kaunda of Zambia and Julius Nyerere of Tanzania. Their actions convinced Thatcher that recognition of Zimbabwe-Rhodesia would result in the downfall of the Commonwealth and severe economic (oil) pressure on Great Britain.

7. Smith, 313.

8. Cilliers, 55.

9. Smith, 321. "Mugabe believed that he had not gained sufficient concessions to ensure his victory in the election, and so he decided to register his protest by making a dramatic withdrawal from the conference. He had packed his bags and was making arrangements to fly out to the United States" Machel informed Mugabe that if he broke away from the conference, he would not be permitted to continue using Mozambique as a base for his operations. Mugabe, chastened, returned to the conference.

10. Binda, *Masodja*, 371.

11. Frangible tank munitions, or "frantan" were Rhodesian made napalm canisters.

12. A *dwala* is a large rock formation, in Chishona.

13. Binda, *Masodja*, 371-2.
14. Binda, *Masodja*, 372.
15. Binda.
16. Binda, *Masodja*, 372-3.
17. Bell UH-1 helicopters snuck into Rhodesia late in the war to replace the aging fleet of Allouettes were called "Cheetahs."
18. Binda, *Masodja*, 374.
19. Binda, *Masodja*, 365-6.
20. CF20110922M0001, former RAR and SAS officer, interview by author, Reading, England.
21. Wood, *Counterstrike*, 48.
22. Binda, *Masodja*, 383; Martin, 330.
23. CF20110920S0001, former RAR officer, interview.
24. Binda, *Masodja*, 383; CE20110913M0001, former RAR officer, interview.
25. CE20110913M0001, former RAR officer, interview.
26. Binda, *Masodja*, 383-4; Moorcraft, 182.
27. Binda, *Masodja*, 384.
28. Binda.
29. Binda, *Masodja*, 384.
30. Binda, 385.
31. Binda, 385-6.
32. The armored car used by the Rhodesian Army was the Eland 90 Mk9, a South African variant of the French made AML Panhard. The Eland was a wheeled (4x4) vehicle armed primarily with a 90mm gun and a 60mm breech-loading mortar.
33. CF20111116J0001, email correspondence with the author, 16 November 2011.
34. CF20111116J0001.
35. Binda, *Masodja*, 388-9. From a statement by 2nd Lt. John Hopkins, A Company 1RAR.
36. CF20110920V0001, former RAR officer, interview.
37. CE20110913M0001, former RAR officer, interview.
38. CE20110913M0001; CE20110920S001, former RAR officer, interview by author.

Chapter 8
Conclusions

> Since the birth of the Regiment I have known it. Since its formation I have done what I could to teach these men of the Rhodesian African Rifles. I have seen the glorious results of that teaching of mine and of the officers of the Regiment.
>
> And today we all smile together. For have we not fought and risked our lives side by side to keep our land safe from the horrible things we have seen here? And the war being over, we feel that we may think of our fighting comrades and-having seen what war can cause to people and to lands-may humbly say *Ishe Komborera Africa* [God save Africa].
>
> — RSM Stephen Machado, 1RAR,
> written after returning from Burma in 1945

This study of the RAR reveals several points about the Rhodesian Bush War that have been largely missed in previous accounts. Many of the existing histories of Rhodesia discount the important role of black soldiers in the Rhodesian Army-some flatly fail to acknowledge that, particularly towards the end of the war, most of the Rhodesian Security Forces were black. In the RAR, the Rhodesian government had a historical demonstration of blacks and whites working together-a true non-racial organization, and a model for cooperation across cultures. Many critiques of Rhodesia's transition to majority rule state that it was a case of "too little, too late." The tragic truth of this also applies to the RAR: throughout the war, there were not enough RAR battalions, and the realization that more black soldiers-and black officers-were needed occurred far too late in the war, despite early recommendations from the Rhodesian Army as early as 1963.

Throughout its history, and particularly during the Bush War, the soldiers of the RAR remained unquestioningly loyal and faithful to their regiment. The soldiers of the RAR were well trained, well-disciplined and feared by their enemy. They were respected by nearly every soldier who ever worked with them. They overcame precisely the same racial and tribal divisions that tore their country apart with an identity of their own-a regimental culture that demanded the best of its members, black and white.

Why did The RAR fight?

The RAR never suffered for recruits. By one officer's recollection, at the end of war, 11 Infantry Battalion (1RAR) was at full strength, with 1,505 soldiers, all the same soldiers who fought for Rhodesia.[1]

The other battalions were similarly fully manned. The regiment never had to leave its base to conduct recruiting drives. They would simply announce what days they were open to recruits, and volunteers came to the depot in droves.

Young black men knew the regiment-their fathers served in it, as did their grandfathers. The pay and living arrangements, while far inferior to those of white soldiers, made the RAR a lucrative job for a black Rhodesian. The RAR uniform was something of which he could be justly proud. Once they arrived at the RAR for training, however, the traditions and mindset of the regiment began to manifest themselves in the actions of the young soldiers. Recruits were taught exactly what their predecessors had done, and what was expected of them, through traditions handed down from long-ago service with the British Army. This instruction built three basic values of the RAR soldier: loyalty, pride, and discipline. These values made the RAR a formidable force on the Rhodesian battlefield.

How Did The RAR change through the war?

At the beginning of the war, the RAR was still very linked to its past as a colonial British unit. That link never really faded. The badge, colors, uniform, and structure remained throughout the war. Even at Entumbane in 1981, the RAR still wore their Rhodesian patches and badge. However, over the course of the Bush War, some of the formalities of British African units fell away. Formal social gatherings were rare by the end of the Bush War, as officers spent more time training and deploying than socializing. Parades and drill instruction were not emphasized as heavily as marksmanship and patrolling.

While the RAR conducted relatively few external raids, they showed that they were capable of doing so. Instead, the regiment tended to focus on internal operations-that is, operations within Rhodesia to locate and destroy insurgent networks in the *kraals* and tribal areas. The regiment could observe and engage the black population much more naturally and efficiently than their counterparts in the RLI.

Unfortunately, the Rhodesian Army could not act on its own advice in 1963 to form more battalions of RAR, or to equalize pay and commission black officers into the ranks. This would have been a welcome move for the army, but politics prevented it. 2RAR did not form until 1975, and 3RAR not until 1979. Had additional battalions formed earlier in the war-even as late as 1973-the additional black troops might have accomplished the one critical task that Rhodesian strategy failed to address—they might have connected more of the black population with the government of Rhodesia.

The creation, late in the war, of Guard Force and Security Force Auxiliaries (*pfomu re vanhu*) indicate a belated attempt to secure the Protected Villages and tribal areas from insurgent infiltration. However, as the RAR well knew, properly trained forces took time to create. Earlier commitment of additional battalions of RAR to this task may have prevented the dismal failure of the PV program, and enabled the Rhodesian government to avoid the forced use of political militias such as the SFAs.

What happened to the RAR?

When the regiment disbanded, most of the RAR soldiers stayed in Zimbabwe. They had nowhere else to go, and most lacked the means to move. Some white officers, committed to helping their new country, also stayed. Most of the white officers, seeing no hope for their future in Zimbabwe, either left for South Africa or Great Britain.

Some of the black soldiers, NCOs and officers who stayed in Zimbabwe continued to serve in the Zimbabwe Army, one former RAR soldier is reported to have become a Lieutenant Colonel, eventually commanding 11 Infantry Battalion (formerly 1RAR).[2] In 2007, four former RAR soldiers came to London for the release of the Regimental History, *Masodja*. When reunited with their former officers, these men were overcome with emotion, as were the officers. There was no hatred or anger between these men and the whites who left.[3]

In the end, the legacy of the RAR is the creation of a multicultural organization that stood the test of tremendous pressure as the nation it served changed, struggled, and ultimately collapsed. Despite the violent changes in the world around it, the regiment stood until it was forced to abandon its link to past traditions and merge into the ranks of the Zimbabwe Army.

What does this mean?

As of the writing of this paper the US military is involved in developing military organizations to build and maintain stability in Iraq and Afghanistan. The role of the US military in developing and assisting African militaries is also increasing, after the 2008 establishment of US Africa Command. These examples share the challenges that the RAR successfully overcame. The challenges of creating a national army out of Tajik, Pashtu, and Dari cultures, or Sunni and Shia tribes in Iraq, or any number of tribes in any African country, is not unlike the RAR's challenge of uniting its white, Ndebele, and Shona cultures into a cohesive and effective unit. The success of the RAR resided in its creation of an overriding concept-the regiment-to which every soldier bound himself above all other divisive elements of his background. Properly developed and maintained, military culture, based on loyalty to the regiment, can be a catalyst to unite disparate cultural groups of soldiers.

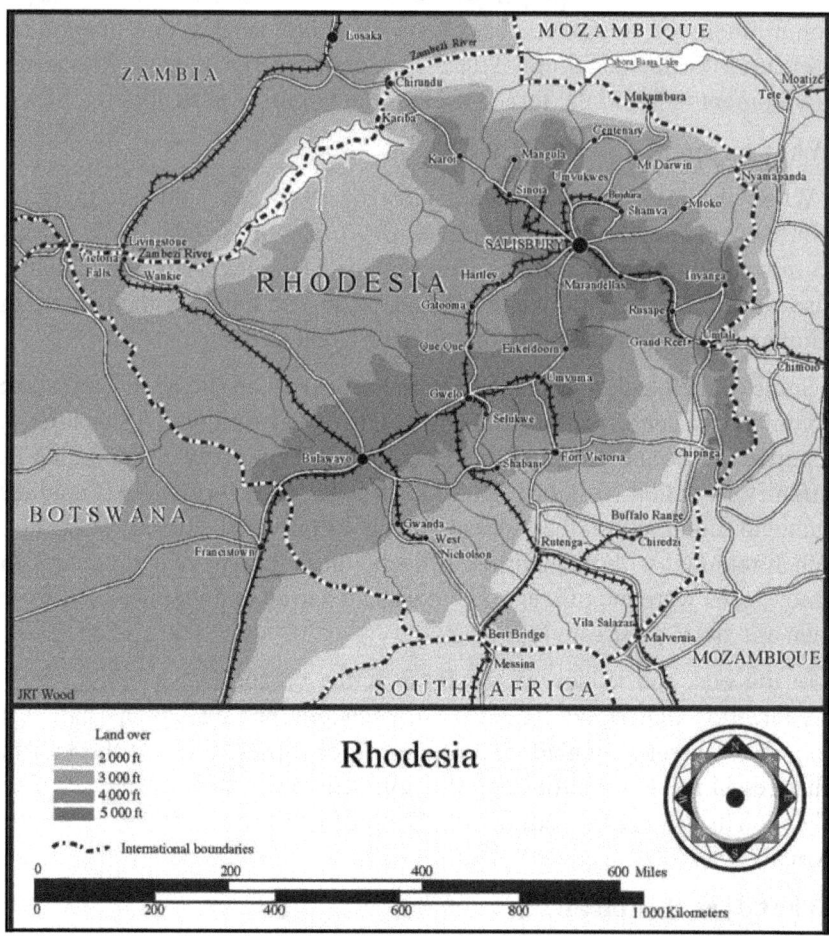

Figure 1. Map of Rhodesia.
Source: Courtesy of Dr. J. R. T. Wood.

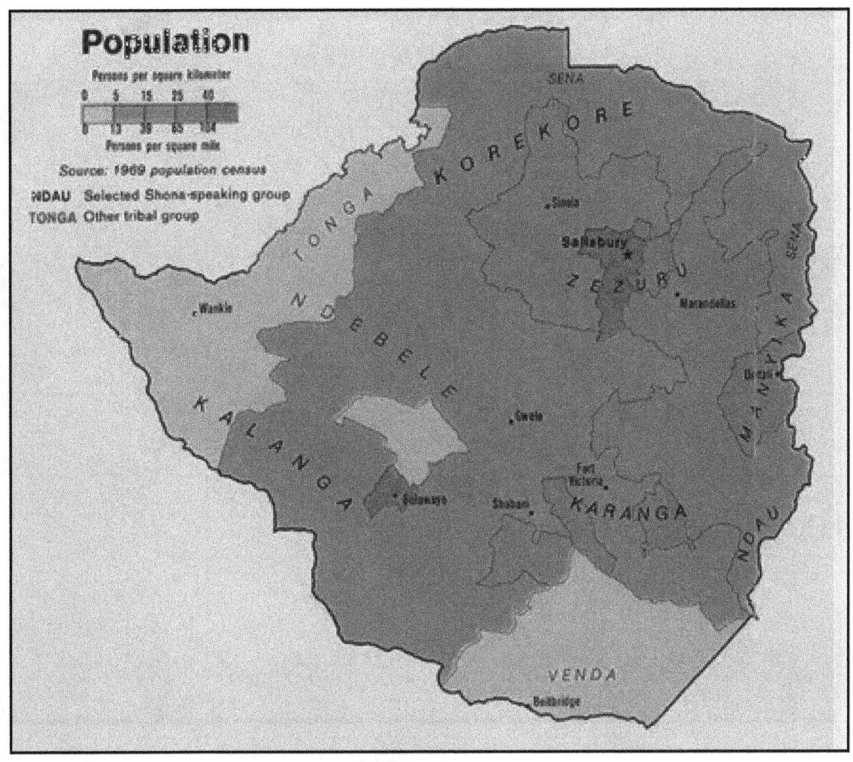

Figure 2. Rhodesian population, 1969.

Source: 1969 Census data, as found at: http://mappery.com/South-Rhodesia-Population-Map (accessed 10 October 2011).

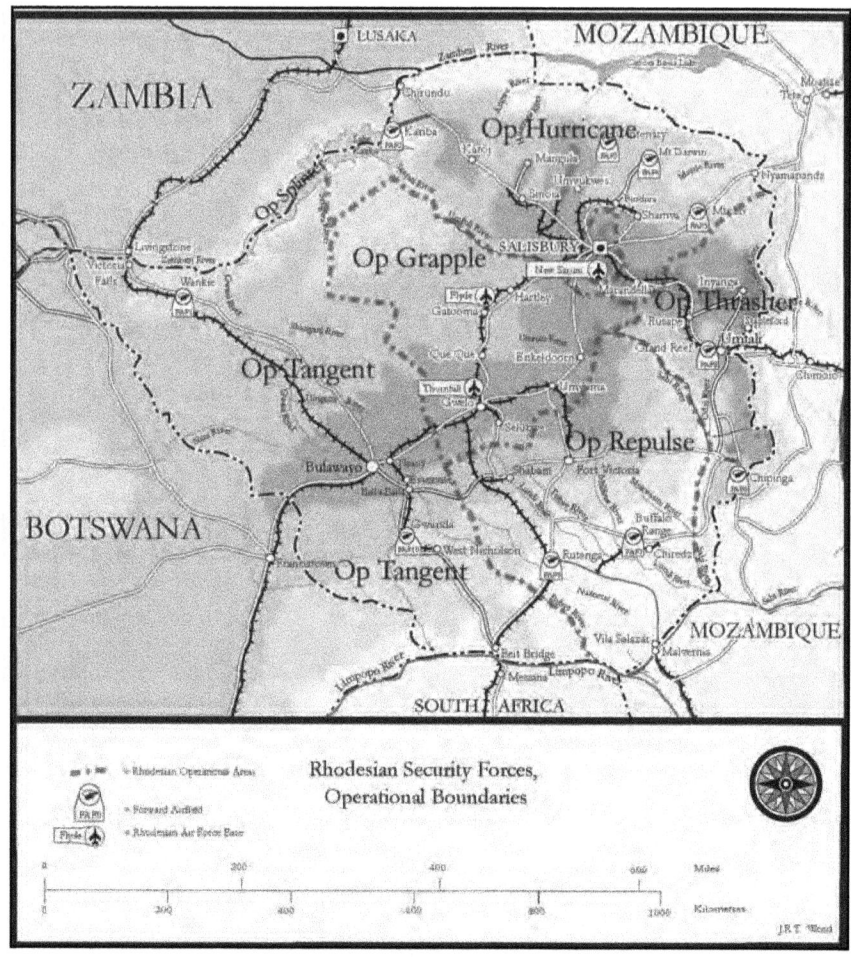

Figure 3. Rhodesian Security Forces Operational Boundaries.
Source: Courtesy of Dr. J. R. T. Wood.

Notes
1. CE20110913M0001, former RAR officer, interview.
2. CF20110920S0001, former RAR officer, interview.
3. CF20110920H0001, former RAR officer, interview.

Bibliography

Primary Sources

Interviews

Command and General Staff College (CGSC) Scholars Program 2011. Scholars Program Art of War Research Study 2011. Research Study, Fort Leavenworth, KS: Ike Skelton Chair in the Art of War, 2011. This study included interviews of counterinsurgency practitioners and policy professionals from the United States, United Kingdom, and South Africa. Each interview was executed as an oral history interview and adhered to Army policies of informed consent in compliance with federal law. Finally, each interview was coordinated throught the Ike Skelton Chair in the Art of War, CGSC Fort Leavenworth, KS.

Johannesburg, Republic of South Africa

CE20110908G0001. Former RAR officer. Interview by author, 8 September 2011.

CE20110908W0001. Former RAR and SAS officer. Interview by author, 8 September 2011.

CE20110908M0001. Former RAR officer. Interview by author, 8 September 2011.

CE20110909R0001. Former RAR officer. Interview by author, 9 September 2011.

CE20110910T0001. Former RAR officer. Interview by author, 9 September 2011.

CE20110910H0001. Former NRR and RAR officer. Interview by author, 10 September 2011.

Durban, Republic of South Africa

CE20110910W0001. Former RR NCO and officer. Interview by author, 10 September 2011.

CE20110912A0001. Former RLI officer. Interview by author, 12 September 2011.

CE20110912G0001. Former Royal Gurkha Rifles and RAR officer. Interview by author, 12 September 2011.

CE20110912G0001. Former BSAP, RRR and RAR officer. Interview by author, 12 September 2011.

CE20110913B0001. Former RAR officer. Interview by author, 13 September 2011.

CE20110913M0001. Former KAR, RAR and Grey's Scouts officer. Interview by author, 13 September 2011.

Cape Town, Republic of South Africa

CE20110913R0001. Former RAR and SAS officer. Interview by author, 13 September 2011.

CE20110914B0001. Former KAR, RLI, and RAR officer. Interview by author, 14 September 2011.

CE20110914H0001. Former RAR Warrant Officer. Interview by author, 14 September 2011.

CE20110915C0001. Former RAR, Royal Gurkha Rifles, and SAS officer. Interview by author, 15 September 2011.

CE20110915B0001. Former RAR and SAS officer. Interview by author, 15 September 2011.

CE20110916G0001. Former RAR officer. Interview by author, 16 September 2011.

CE20110916M0001. Former RAR and SAS officer. Interview by author, 16 September 2011.

Aylesford, England

CF20110919C0001. Former RAR officer. Interview by author, 19 September 2011.

CF20110919H0001. Former RRR, RAR, and Rhodesian Army Education Corps officer. Interview by author, 19 September 2011.

CF20110919W0001. Former RLI and RAR officer. Interview by author, 19 September 2011.

London, England

CF20110920H0001. Former RAR officer. Interview by author, 20 September 2011.

CF20110920S0001. Former KAR, RAR officer. Interview by author, 20 September 2011.

CF20110920V0001. Former RAR officer. Interview by author, 20 September 2011.

Reading, England

CF20110922L0001. Former British Army, RAR officer. Interview by author, 22 September 2011.

CF20110922L0002. Former RAR, British Army officer. Interview by author, 22 September 2011.

CF20110922M0001. Former RAR, SAS officer. Interview by author, 22 September 2011.

Portland, Oregon

CG20110927S0001. Former U. S. Special Forces, RAR officer. Interview by author, 27 September 2011.

Fort Leavenworth, Kansas

CB20111110S0001. Former Selous Scouts officer. Interview by author, 10 November 2011.

Personal Accounts

Croukamp, Dennis. *The Bush War in Rhodesia: An Extraordinary Combat Memoir of a Rhodesian Reconnaissance Specialist*. Boulder, CO: Paladin Press, 2007.

Cox, Chris. *Fireforce: One Man's War in the Rhodesian Light Infantry*. Johannesburg: 30 Degrees South, 2006.

Essex-Clark, John. *Maverick Soldier: An Infantryman's Story*. Carlton: Melbourne University Press, 1991.

Lemon, David. *Never Quite a Soldier: A Rhodesian Policeman's War 1971-1982*. Alberton: Galago, 2006.

Mills, Greg, and Grahame Wilson. "Who Dares Loses? Assessing Rhodesia's Counter-Insurgency Experience." *RUSI* 152, no. 6 (December 2007): 22-31.

Smith, Ian Douglas. *The Great Betrayal: The Memoirs of Ian Douglas Smith*. London: Blake, 1997.

Warren, Charlie. *Stick Leader: RLI*. South Africa: Just Done Productions, 2007.

Wood, J. R. T. *The War Diaries of André Dennison*. Gibraltar: Ashanti, 1989.

Documents

DesFountain, Trevor. Summary and Background of 1979 Rhodesian Strategy Revision Conference.

Essex-Clark, John. "The Incorrigible Trio~A Subaltern's View: A Controversial Essay in Bonding, Leadership, and Morale."

Marillier, Ron. "A Short History of the 3d Battalion Rhodesian African Rifles."

National Security Council. *Study In Response to National Security Study Memorandum 39: Southern Africa.* Washington, DC, 9 December 1969.

Redfern, John. "Racial Discrimination in the Rhodesia and Nyasaland Army." Rhodesian Army memorandum, October 1962.

———. "The Requirement for a Non-Racial Army in Southern Rhodesia." Rhodesian Army memorandum, October 1963.

Doctrinal References

Department of the Army. FM 3-24, *Counterinsurgency.* Washington DC: Government Printing Office, 2006.

Rhodesian Army. COIN Manual, Part II—ATOPS [Anti-Terrorist Operations]. Salisbury, 1975.

Secondary Sources

Andrade, Dale. "Westmoreland was right: Learning the wrong lessons from the Vietman War." *Small Wars and Insurgencies* 19, no. 2 (June 2008): 145-181.

Bergerud, Eric. *The Dynamics of Defeat: The Vietnam War in Hau Nghia Province.* Oxford: Westview Press, 1991.

Binda, Alexandre. *Masodja: The History of the Rhodesian African Rifles and its forerunner, the Rhodesia Native Regiment.* Johannesburg: 30 Degrees South, 2007.

———. *The Saints: The Rhodesian Light Infantry.* Edited by Chris Cocks. Johannesburg: 30 Degrees South, 2007.

Bridgland, Fred. "Angola and the West." In *Challenge: Southern Africa within the African Revolutionary context,* edited by Al J. Ventner, 117-145. Gibraltar: Ashanti, 1989.

Burton, Brian, and John Nagl. "Learning as we go: the US Army adapts to COIN in Iraq." *Small Wars and Insurgencies* 19, no. 3 (September 2008): 303-327.

Cann, John P. *Counterinsurgency in Africa: The Portuguese Way of War, 1961-1974.* Westport, CT: Greenwood Press, 1997.

Cilliers, J. K. *Counter-insurgency in Rhodesia.* London: Croom Helm, 1985.

Clayton, Anthony. *Counterinsurgency in Kenya: A study of military operations against the Mau Mau, 1952-1960.* Manhattan, KS: Sunflower University Press, 1976.

Coates, John. *Suppressing Insurgency.* Boulder, CO: Westview Press, 1992.

Cole, Barbara. *The Elite: The story of the Rhodesian Special Air Service.* South Africa: 1985.

Comber, Leon. *Malaya's Secret Police 1945-1960: The Role of the Special Branch in the Malayan Emergency.* Melbourne: Monash University Press, 2009.

Corum, James. "Training Indigenous Forces in Counterinsurgency: A Tale of Two Insurgencies." March 2006. http://www.strategicstudiesinstitute.army.mil/pubs/display.cfm?PubID=648 (accessed 20 June 2011).

Dobbins, James, Seth G. Jones, Keith Crane, Andrew Rathnell, Brett Steele, Richard Teltshik, and Anga Timilsina. *The UN's Role in Nation-Building: From the Congo to Iraq.* Santa Monica, CA: RAND, 2005.

Dornan Jr., James E., ed. *Rhodesia Alone.* Washington, DC: Council on American Affairs, 1977.

Downie, Nick, and Lord Richard Cecil. *Frontline Rhodesia.* DVD. Johannesburg: 30 Degrees South, 2007.

Farwell, Byron. *Mr. Kipling's Army.* New York: W. W. Norton, 1981.

Gann, Lewis H., and Thomas H. Henriksen. *The Struggle for Zimbabwe: Battle in the Bush.* New York: Praeger, 1981.

Galula, David. *Counterinsurgency Warfare: Theory and Practice.* London: Praeger Security International, 1964, 2006.

———. *Pacification in Algeria 1956-1958.* Santa Monica, CA: RAND, 2006.

Gentile, Gian. "A strategy of tactics: population centric COIN and the Army." *Parameters* (Autumn 2009): 5-17.

Green, T. N. *The Guerilla - Selections from the Marine Corps Gazette.* New York: Praeger.

Hack, Karl. "The Malayan Emergency as a Counter-Insurgency Paradigm." *The Journal of Strategic Studies* 32, no. 3 (June 2009): 383-414.

Hammes, Thomas X. *The Sling and the Stone: On War in the 21st Century.* St. Paul, MN: Zenith Press, 2006.

Henniker, M. C. A. *Red Shadow Over Malaya.* London: William Blackwood and Sons, 1955.

Hoffman, Bruce. *Lessons for Contemporary Counterinsurgencies: The Rhodesian Experience.* Santa Monica : RAND, 1992.

Hoffman, Frank. "Neo-Classical Counterinsurgency?" *Parameters* (Summer 2007): 71-87.

Hoffman, Frank, Jennifer M. Taw, and David Arnold. *Lessons for Contemporary Counterinsurgencies: The Rhodesian Experience.* Santa Monica, CA: RAND, 1991.

Hopkinson, Michael. *The Irish War of Independence.* Montreal: McGill-Queen's University Press, 2002.

Horne, Alistair. "The French Army and the Algerian War 1954-62." In *Regular Armies and Insurgency*, edited by Ronald Haycock, 69-83. London: Croom Helm, 1979.

Hunt, Richard. *Pacification: The American Struggle for Vietnam's Hearts and Minds.* Boulder, CO: Westview Press, 1995.

Hyam, Ronald. *Britain's Declining Empire: The Road to Decolonisation, 1918-1968.* Cambridge: Cambridge University Press, 2006.

Jeudwine, Hugh. "A Record of the Rebellion in Ireland in 1920-1, and the Part Played by the Army in Dealing with it (Intelligence)." In *British Intelligence in Ireland: The Final Reports*, edited by Peter Hart, 17-60. Cork: Cork University Press, 2002.

Kempton, Daniel R. *Soviet Strategy Toward Southern Africa: The National Liberation Movement Connection.* New York: Praeger, 1989.

Kilcullen, David J. *The Accidental Guerilla: Fighting Small Wars in the Midst of a Big One.* Oxford: Oxford University Press, 2009.

———. *Counterinsurgency.* Oxford: Oxford University Press, 2010.

Kitson, Frank. *Bunch of Five.* London: Faber and Faber, 1977.

Komer, Robert. *Bureaucracy at War: US Performance in the Vietnam Conflict.* Boulder, CO: Westview Press, 1986.

———. *The Malayan Emergency in Retrospect: Organization of a Successful Counterinsurgency Effort*. Santa Monica, CA: RAND, 1972.

Krepinevich, Andrew. *The Army and Vietnam*. Baltimore, MD: Johns Hopkins University Press, 1986.

Kriger, Norma. *Zimbabwe's Guerilla War: Peasant Voices*. Cambridge: Cambridge University Press, 1992.

Lockhart, J. G., and The Hon. C. M. Woodhouse. *Cecil Rhodes: The Colossus of Southern Africa*. New York: Macmillan, 1963.

Lunt, James. *Imperial Sunset: Frontier Soldiering in the 20th Century*. London: Macdonald Futura, 1981.1

MacKinlay, John. "Rethinking Counterinsurgency." *RAND Counterinsurgency Study*, Volume 5, 2008.

———. *The Insurgent Archipelago*. London: C Hurst and Co Publishers Ltd., 2009.

Malkasian, Carter, and Daniel Marston, eds. *Counterinsurgency in Modern Warfare*. Oxford: Osprey Publishing, 2010.

Martin, David, and Phyllis Johnson. *The Struggle for Zimbabwe: The Chimurenga War*. London: Faber and Faber, 1981.

McCuen, John. *The Art of Counter-Revolutionary War*. Harrisburg, PA: Stockpole Books, 1966.

Miers, Richard. *Shoot to Kill*. London: Faber and Faber, 1959.

Minford, John. *Sun Tzu The Art of War: The Essential Translation of the Classic Book of Life*. New York: Penguin Press, 2002.

Moorcraft, Paul L., and Peter McLaughlin. *The Rhodesian War: A Military History*. Johannesburg: Jonathan Ball, 1982.

Nagl, John. *Counterinsurgency Lessons from Malaya and Vietnam: Learning to Eat Soup with a Knife*. Westport, CT: Praeger, 2002.

Nyangoni, Wellington W. *African Nationalism in Zimbabwe (Rhodesia)*. Washington, DC: University Press of America, 1977.

O'Meara, Patrick. *Rhodesia: Racial Conflict or Coexistence?* Ithaca: Cornell University Press, 1975.

Owen, Christopher. *The Rhodesian African Rifles*. Edited by Lt.-General Sir Brian Horrocks. London: Leo Cooper, 1970.

Paret, Peter. *French Revolutionary Warfare from Indochina to Algeria: The Analysis of a Political and Military Doctrine*. London: Pall Mall Press, 1964.

Phillips, Rufus. *Why Vietnam Matters: An Eyewitness Account of lessons not learned*. Annapolis, MD: Naval Institute Press, 2008.

Porch, Douglas. "Bugeaud, Gallieni, Lyautey: The Development of French Colonial Warfare." In *Makers of Modern Strategy*, edited by Peter Paret, 376-407. Princeton, NJ: Princeton University Press, 1986.

———. "French Imperial Warfare 1945-62." In *Counterinsurgency in Modern Warfare*, edited by Daniel Marston and Carter Malkasian, 87-101. Oxford: Osprey Publishing, 2010.

Race, Jeffrey. *War Comes to Long An*. California: UC Press, 1972.

Ramsey, Robert. *Savage Wars of Peace: Case Studies of Pacification in the Philippines, 1900-1902*. Fort Leavenworth, KS: Combat Studies Institute, 2007.

Reed, Douglas. *The Battle for Rhodesia*. New York: Devin-Adair, 1967.

Reid-Daly, Ron. *Selous Scouts: Top Secret War*. Cape Town: Galago, 1983.

———. "War in Rhodesia--Cross-Border Operations." In *Challenge: Southern Africa within the African Revolutionary context,* edited by Al J. Ventner, 146-182. Gibraltar: Ashanti, 1989.

Scully, Pat. *Exit Rhodesia*. Ladysmith: Cottswold Press, 1984.

Shy, John, and Thomas Collier. "Revolutionary War." In *Makers of Modern Strategy*, edited by Peter Paret, 815-862. Princeton, NJ: Princeton University Press, 1986.

Sibanda, Eliakim M. *The Zimbabwe African People's Union 1961-87: A Political History of Insurgency in Southern Rhodesia*. Trenton: Africa World Press, 2005.

Smith, Simon. "General Templer and Counter-insurgency in Malaya: Hearts and Minds, intelligence, and propaganda." *Intelligence and National Security* 16, no. 3: 60-78.

Sobel, Lester A., ed. *Rhodesia / Zimbabwe 1971-77*. New York: Facts On File, 1978.

Stiff, Peter. *Cry Zimbabwe: Independence - Twenty Years On*. Alberton: Galago, 2000.

Stubbs, Richard. "From Search and Destroy to Hearts and Minds: The Evolution of British Strategy in Malaya 1948-1960." In *Counterinsurgency in Modern Warfare*, edited by Daniel Marston and Carter Malkasian, 101-118. Oxford: Osprey Publishing, 2010.

Sutherland, Riley. *Army Operations in Malaya, 1947-1960*. Santa Monica CA: RAND, 1964.

Thompson, Robert. *Defeating Communist Insurgency*. London: Chatto and Windhus, 1966.

Thompson, W. Scott, and Donaldson Frizzell, eds. *The Lessons of Vietnam*. New York: Crane, Russak and Company, 1977.

Trinquier, Roger. *Modern Warfare: A French View of Counterinsurgency*. Fort Leavenworth, KS: CSI, 1985.

Tse-Tung, Mao. *On Guerilla Warfare*. New York: Dover Publications, 2005.

Ucko, David. *The New Counterinsurgency Era: Transforming the US Military for Modern Wars*. Washington, DC: Georgetown University Press, 2009.

Ventner, Al J. ed. *Challenge: Southern Africa within the African Revolutionary context*. Gibraltar: Ashanti, 1989.

———. *The Chopper Boys: Helicopter Warfare in Africa*. London: Greenhill, 1994.

Willbanks, James. *Abandoning Vietnam*. Lawrence, KS: University of Kansas Press, 2004.

Wood, J. R. T. "Countering the CHIMURENGA: The Rhodesian Counterinsurgency Campaign." In *Counterinsurgency in Modern Warfare*, edited by Daniel Marston and Carter Malkasian, 191-208. Oxford: Osprey Publishing, 2010.

———. *Counterstrike From the Sky: The Rhodesian All-Arms Fireforce in the War in the Bush 1974-1980*. South Africa: 30 Degrees South Publishers, 2009.

———. "Counter-punching on the Mudzi: D Company, 1st Rhodesian African Rifles, on operation 'Mardon' 1 November 1976." *Small Wars and Insurgencies* 9, no. 2 (Autumn 1998): 64-82.

www.ingramcontent.com/pod-product-compliance
Lightning Source LLC
Chambersburg PA
CBHW050502110426
42742CB00018B/3344